Practicing Organization Development

**The Change Agent Series
for Groups and Organizations**

MISSION STATEMENT

The books in this series are intended to be cutting-edge, state-of-the-art, and innovative approaches to participative change in organizational settings. They are written for, and written by, organization development (OD) practitioners interested in new approaches to facilitating participative change. They are geared to providing both theory and advice on practical application.

SERIES EDITORS

**William J. Rothwell
Roland Sullivan
Kristine Quade**

EDITORIAL BOARD

**David Bradford
W. Warner Burke
Edie Seashore
Robert Tannenbaum
Christopher Worley
Shaolin Zhang**

Facilitating Organization Change

Lessons from Complexity Science

Edwin E. Olson
Glenda H. Eoyang

Forewords by Richard Beckhard and Peter Vaill

JOSSEY-BASS/PFEIFFER
A Wiley Company
San Francisco

Practicing
Organization
Development

Copyright © 2001 by Jossey-Bass/Pfeiffer
Jossey-Bass/Pfeiffer is a registered trademark of Jossey-Bass Inc., A Wiley Company.
ISBN: 0-7879-5330-X

Library of Congress Cataloging-in-Publication Data

Olson, Edwin E.
   Facilitating organization change : lessons from complexity
science / Edwin E. Olson, Glenda H. Eoyang ; foreword by Peter
Vaill.
      p. cm. — (Practicing organization development series)
Includes bibliographical references and index.
   ISBN 0-7879-5330-X
   1. Organizational change. I. Eoyang, Glenda H. II. Title. III.
Series.
   HD58.8 .O47 2001
   658.4'092—dc21

                          00-011521

Printed in the United States of America.

Published by

JOSSEY-BASS/PFEIFFER
A Wiley Company
350 Sansome Street, 5th Floor
San Francisco, CA 94104-1342
415.433.1740; Fax 415.433.0499
800.274.4434; Fax 800.569.0443

www.pfeiffer.com

Acquiring Editor: Matthew Holt
Director of Development: Kathleen Dolan Davies
Developmental Editor: Susan Rachmeler
Editor: Rebecca Taff

Senior Production Editor: Dawn Kilgore
Manufacturing Manager: Becky Carreño
Interior and Cover Design: Bruce Lundquist
Illustrations: Richard Sheppard

Printing   10 9 8 7 6 5 4 3 2 1

 This book is printed on acid-free, recycled stock that meets or exceeds the minimum GPO and EPA requirements for recycled paper.

Contents

List of Tables, Figures, and Exhibits

Foreword
to the Series

ON **1967,** Warren Bennis, Ed Schein, and I were faculty members of the Sloan School of Management at MIT. We decided to produce a series of paperback books that collectively would describe the state of the field of organization development (OD). Organization development as a field had been named by myself and several others from our pioneer change effort at General Mills in Minneapolis, Minnesota, some ten years earlier.

Today I define OD as "a systemic and systematic change effort, using behavioral science knowledge and skill, to transform the organization to a new state."

In any case, several books and many articles had been written, but there was no consensus on whether OD was a field of practice, an area of study, or a profession. We had not even established OD as a theory or even as a practice.

We decided that there was a need for something that would describe the state of OD. Our intention was to each write a book and also to recruit three other authors. After some searching, we found a young editor who had just joined the small publishing house of Addison-Wesley. We made contact, and the series was born. Our audience was to be human resource professionals who spent their time consulting with managers in their development through various small-group activities, such as team building. More than thirty books have been published in that series, and the series has had a life of its own. We just celebrated its thirtieth anniversary.

At last year's National OD Network Conference, I said that it was time for the OD profession to change and transform itself. Is that not what we change agents tell our clients to do? This new Jossey-Bass/Pfeiffer series will do just that. It can be seen as:

- A documentation of the re-invention of OD;

- An effort that will take us to the next level; and

- A practical effort to transfer to the world the theory and practice of leading-edge practitioners and theorists.

The books in this new series will thus prove to be valuable resources for change agents to keep current with the new and leading-edge ideas and practices.

May this very exciting change agent series be most creative and innovative. May it give our field a renewed burst of energy and awareness.

Richard Beckhard
Written on Labor Day weekend 1999 from my summer cabin near Bethel, Maine

Introduction
to the Series

"We must become the change we want to see."

—*Mahatma Gandhi*

"We live in a moment of history where change is so speeded up that we begin to see the present only when it is already disappearing."

—*R. D. Laing*

WE CAN EXPECT MORE CHANGE to occur in our lifetimes than has occurred since the beginning of civilization over ten thousand years ago. *Practicing Organization Development: The Change Agent Series for Groups and Organizations* is a new series of books being launched to help those who must cope with or create change in organizational settings. That includes almost everyone.

The Current State of Organization Development

Our view of OD in this series is an optimistic one. We believe that OD is gaining favor as decision makers realize that a balance *must* be struck between the drivers of change and the people involved in it and affected by it. Although OD does have its disadvantages at a time characterized by quantum leap change, it remains preferable to such alternative approaches to change as coercion, persuasion, leadership change, and debate.[1] Organization development practitioners are reinventing their approaches, based on certain foundational roots of the field, in combination with emerging principles to ensure that OD will increasingly be recognized as a viable, important, and inherently participative approach to help people in organizations facilitate, anticipate, and manage change.

A Brief History of the Genesis of the OD Series

A few years ago, and as a direct result of the success of *Practicing Organization Development: A Guide for Practitioners* by Rothwell, Sullivan, and McLean, the publisher—feeling that OD was experiencing a rebirth of interest in the United States and in other nations—wanted to launch a new OD series. The goal of this new series was not to replace, or even compete directly with, the well-established Addison-Wesley OD Series (edited by Edgar Schein). Instead, as the editors saw it, this series would provide a means by which the most promising authors in OD whose voices had not previously been heard could share their ideas. The publisher enlisted the support of Bill Rothwell, Roland Sullivan, and Kristine Quade to turn the dream of a series into a reality.

This series was long in the making. After sharing many discussions with the publisher and circulating among themselves several draft descriptions of the series editorial guidelines, the editors were guests of Bob Tannenbaum, one of the field's founders, in Carmel, California, in February 1999 to discuss the series with a group of well-known OD practitioners interested in authoring books. Several especially supportive publisher representatives, including Matt Holt and Josh Blatter, were also present at that weekend-long meeting. It was an opportunity for diverse OD practitioners, representing many philosophical viewpoints, to come together to share their vision for a new book series. In a sense, this series represents an OD intervention in the OD field in that it is geared to bringing change to the field most closely associated with change management and facilitation.

---

[1]W. Rothwell, R. Sullivan, & G. McLean. (1995). Introduction (pp. 3–46). In W. Rothwell, R. Sullivan, & G. McLean, *Practicing Organization Development: A Guide for Consultants.* San Francisco, CA: Jossey-Bass/ Pfeiffer.

What Distinguishes the Books in this Series

The books in this series are meant to be cutting-edge and state-of-the-art in their approach to OD. The goal of the series is to provide an outlet for proven authorities in OD who have not put their ideas into print or for up-and-coming writers in OD who have new, sometimes unorthodox, approaches that are stimulating and exciting. Some of the books in this series describe inspirational concepts that can lead to actionable change and purvey ideas so new that they are not fully developed.

Unique to this series is the cutting-edge emphasis, the immediate applicability, and the ease of transferability of the concepts. The aim of this series is nothing less than to reinvent, re-energize, and reinvigorate OD. In each book, we have also recommended that the author(s) provide:

- A research base of some kind, meaning new information derived from practice and/or systematic investigation and

- Practical tools, worksheets, case studies and other ready-to-go approaches that help the authors drag "theory" to "practice" to make these new, cutting-edge approaches more concrete.

Subject Matter That Will (and Will Not) Be Covered

The books in this series are varied in their approach, but they are united by their focus. All share an emphasis on organization development (OD). Hence, books in this series are about participative change efforts. They are not about such other popular topics as leadership, management development, consulting, group dynamics—unless those topics are treated in new, cutting-edge ways and are geared to OD practitioners.

This Book

Rapid, unpredictable change puts pressure on facilitators and leaders of organization change to meet the demands of the marketplace. Olson and Eoyang present a new lens, based on the science of complex adaptive systems, that enables leaders and consultants to recognize environmental changes more clearly, re-engineer organizations on the spot, and increase the degree of "fit" between organization outputs and marketplace demands. The authors answer the following questions: (1) What conditions are required for organizations to self-organize? and (2) How can facilitators help organizations move toward self-organizing conditions? The concepts, examples, and tools presented in this book demonstrate that self-organizing abilities and processes are necessary where the traditional methods of organization change are not successful.

Series Website

For further information and resources about the books in this series and about the current and future practice of organization development, we encourage readers to visit the series website at *www.PracticingOD.com.*

William J. Rothwell
University Park, PA

Roland Sullivan
Deephaven, MN

Kristine Quade
Minnetonka, MN

Statement
of the Board

IT IS OUR PLEASURE TO PARTICIPATE in and influence the start up of *Practicing Organization Development: The Change Agent Series for Groups and Organizations.* The purpose of the series is to stimulate the profession and influence how OD is defined and practiced. This statement is intended to set the context for the series by addressing three important questions: (1) What is OD? (2) Is the OD profession at a crossroads? and (3) What is the purpose of this series?

What Is Organization Development?

We offer the following definition of OD to stimulate debate:

> Organization development is a system-wide and values-based collaborative process of applying behavioral science knowledge to the adaptive development, improvement, and reinforcement of such organizational features as the strategies, structures, processes, people, and cultures that lead to organization effectiveness.

The definition suggests that OD can be understood in terms of its several foci:

First, *OD is a system-wide process.* It works with whole systems. In the past, the bias has been toward working at the individual and group levels. More recently, the focus has shifted to organizations and multi-organization systems. We support that trend in general but honor and acknowledge the fact that the traditional focus on smaller systems is both legitimate and necessary.

Second, *OD is values-based.* Traditionally, OD has attempted to distinguish itself from other forms of planned change and applied behavioral science by promoting a set of humanistic values and by emphasizing the importance of personal growth as a key to its practice. Today, that focus is blurred and there is much debate about the value base underlying the practice of OD. We support a more formal and direct conversation about what these values are and how the field is related to them.

Third, *OD is collaborative.* Our first value commitment as OD practitioners is to bring about an inclusive, diverse workforce with a focus of integrating differences into a world-wide culture mentality.

Fourth, *OD is based on behavioral science knowledge.* Organization development should incorporate and apply knowledge from sociology, psychology, anthropology, technology, and economics toward the end of making systems more effective. We support the continued emphasis in OD on behavioral science knowledge and believe that OD practitioners should be widely read and comfortable with several of the disciplines.

Fifth, *OD is concerned with the adaptive development, improvement, and reinforcement of strategies, structures, processes, people, culture, and other features of organizational life.* This statement not only describes the organizational elements that are the target of change, but also describes the process by which effectiveness is increased. That is, OD works in a variety of areas, and it is focused on improving these areas. We believe that such a statement of process and content strongly implies that a key feature of OD is the transference of knowledge and skill to the system so that it is more able to handle and manage change in the future.

Sixth and finally, *OD is about improving organization effectiveness.* It is not just about making people happy; it is also concerned with meeting financial goals, improving productivity, and addressing stakeholder satisfaction. We believe that OD's future is closely tied to the incorporation of this value in its purpose and the demonstration of this objective in its practice.

Is the OD Profession at a Crossroads?

For years, OD professionals have said that OD is at a crossroads. From our perspective at the beginning of the new millennium, the field of organization development can be characterized by the following statements:

1. Practitioners today are torn. The professional organizations representing OD practitioners, including the OD Network, the OD Institute, the International OD Association, and the Academy of Management's OD and Change Division, are experiencing tremendous uncertainties in their purposes, practices, and relationships.

2. There are increasing calls for regulation/certification.

3. Many respected practitioners have suggested that people who profess to manage change are behind those who are creating it. Organization development practitioners should lead through influence rather than follow the lead of those who are sometimes coercive in their approach to change.

4. The field is defined by techniques.

5. The values that guide the field are unclear and ill-defined.

6. Too many people are practicing OD without any training in the field.

7. Practitioners are having difficulty figuring out how to market their services.

The situation suggests the following provocative questions:

- How can OD practitioners help formulate strategy, shape the strategy development process, contribute to the content of strategy, and drive how strategy will be implemented?

- How can OD practitioners encourage an open examination of the ways organizations are conceived and managed?

- How can OD focus on the drivers of change external to individuals, such as the external environment, business strategy, organization change, and culture change, as well as on the drivers of change internal to individuals, such as individual interpretations of culture, behavior, style, and mind-set?

- How much should OD be part of the competencies of all leaders and how much should it be the sole domain of professionally trained, career-oriented OD practitioners?

What Is the Purpose of This Series?

This series is intended to provide current thinking about OD as a field and to provide practical approaches based on sound theory and research. It is targeted for full-time external or internal OD practitioners; top executives in charge of enterprise-wide change; and managers, HR practitioners, training and development professionals, and others who have responsibility for change in organizational and trans-organizational settings. At the same time, these books will be directed toward cutting-edge thinking and state-of-the-art approaches. In some cases, the ideas, approaches, or techniques described are still evolving, so the books are intended to open up dialogue.

We know that the books in this series will provide a leading forum for thought-provoking dialogue within the OD field.

About the Board Members

David Bradford is senior lecturer in organizational behavior at the Graduate School of Business, Stanford University, Palo Alto, California. He is co-author (with Allan R. Cohen) of *Managing for Excellence, Influence Without Authority*, and *POWER UP: Transforming Organizations Through Shared Leadership*.

W. Warner Burke is professor of psychology and education and chair of the Department of Organization and Leadership at Teachers College, Columbia University, New York, New York. His most recent publication is *Business Profiles of Climate Shifts: Profiles of Change Makers*, (with William Trahant and Richard Koonce).

Edith Whitfield Seashore is organization consultant and co-founder (with Morley Segal) of AUNTL Masters Program in Organization Development. She is co-author of *What Did You Say?* and *The Art of Giving and Receiving Feedback* and co-editor of *The Promise of Diversity*.

Robert Tannenbaum is emeritus professor of development of human systems, Graduate School of Management, University of California, Los Angeles; recipient of Lifetime Achievement Award by the National OD Network. He has published numerous books, including *Human Systems Development* with Newton Margulies and Fred Massarik.

Christopher G. Worley is director, MSOD Program, Pepperdine University, Malibu, California. He is co-author of *Organization Development and Change* (7th ed.), with Tom Cummings, and of *Integrated Strategic Change*, with David Hitchin and Walter Ross.

Shaolin Zhang is senior manager of organization development for Motorola (China) Electronics Ltd. He received his master's degree in American Studies from Beijing Foreign Studies University, Beijing, China, and holds a Ph.D. in sociology from York University, Toronto, Canada.

Foreword

ON THE MID-1990S, an issue of *Fortune* magazine had an unusually arresting cover. It was two pictures, actually—one above the other. The upper picture was of a group of half-dozen or so men in bathing suits, sitting disconsolately with backs to each other on a raft-like contraption that was obviously sinking. The picture below it was of a similar group on a raft, only this time they were happily facing each other as they paddled their buoyant and well-constructed craft across a lake.

The story inside was about new ways of conducting executive development programs in corporations. The two groups on the cover were all executives from one Fortune 50 company. They had each been given identical sets of materials and time limits to build a raft that would take them across a lake. There was only one difference: To build their raft, one team was required to follow all of the company's policies about new product development, planning, budgeting, and organizational structure. The other team—the happy crew of the seaworthy raft—had been left free to proceed in the best way they saw fit.

No doubt both the participants (and more broadly the whole field of executive development) could take many lessons from this experience. It certainly would have been unforgettable; and it is indeed an extremely ingenious exercise. Moreover, it is not an exaggeration to say that, over the years, many similar stories have accumulated, whether as training designs or formal research findings: The lessons are about the power of participation; about the energy that is released when command-control, top-down management is reduced or removed; about the innovations that emerge when formal structures are made more flexible and responsive; and about the capacity of teams to gel around a shared vision and to exhibit extraordinary determination to fulfill that vision.

Experiments with "self-managing teams"—or what in this book are called "self-organizing processes"—have been around Western management practices for forty years or more. Maytag, for example, was building washing machines with five-person teams alongside its 180-person assembly line in the early 1960s. IBM used self-directed teams to build Selectric typewriters in the same years. Volvo famously employed small teams to build whole automobiles, and, in Yugoslavia, workers were designing their own jobs and electing their own supervisors as part of the so-called "industrial democracy" movement. More recently, an entire book of examples of self-managing teams has been published.[1] Probably the most dramatic examples in the entire genre are the "skunk works" that Tom Peters and Bob Waterman discovered and vividly documented in various companies[2]: "If you want high performance from a team," goes the message, "give them the problem, give them a deadline, give them some resources (they'll scrounge a lot more, of course), and leave 'em alone!"

Human innovation, team work, and commitment above and beyond the expected is so impressive and so charming when it occurs, and we have seen it so often, that we may well forget to ask two all-important questions: First, why do self-managing (or self-organizing) groups work at all, let alone so well? And second, how do we help an organization move toward self-organizing conditions, because after years of tight structure and top-down control, it is rarely clear to those involved that removing a lot of the controls and red tape will achieve anything in the longer run but anarchy.

---

[1]Charles C. Manz and Henry P. Sims, Jr., *Business Without Bosses*. New York: John Wiley, 1993.

[2]Thomas J. Peters and Robert H. Waterman, Jr., *In Search of Excellence*. New York: Harper and Row, 1982, p. 211.

Edwin Olson and Glenda Eoyang, the authors of this landmark book, have provided convincing concepts and theory to answer both of these questions. They have made self-organizing abilities and processes, not just one tool in the change consultant's bag, but instead the basis for an entirely new approach to organization change itself. *Self-organizing is the fundamental thing we need to understand and to learn to work with.*

Both authors are experienced organization change consultants, and they know all the traditional theories and practices first-hand. However, in this book they are trying something quite different: They seek to provide the organization change and development field with a new theoretical foundation on which to work with contemporary organizations. As the authors demonstrate thoroughly, present and future organizations will be sailing in waters of unprecedented complexity and instability. The old (what the authors call) "Newtonian" models are simply insufficient for the task.

As noted above with respect to self-managing teams, the organization change and development field—the OD field for short—is no stranger to experiments that try to release energy that is blocked by bureaucratic rigidity and oppressive management. Many ingenious experiments have been tried—to improve lateral communication; break down departmental silos; increase trust among disparate groups; improve the up and down flow of communication through more careful listening; design work that rewards more than mere creature needs; develop structures that are more flexible networks and matrixes; improve the learning climate in order to make the organization more adaptive.

In short, change consultants have indeed been inventive about the contemporary problems of organizational life. But this inventiveness has tended to be ad hoc and intuitive, rather than systematic. Moreover, the change field has not evolved a research tradition by which the various innovations could be reported and reflected on in a systematic and cumulative way. Finally, I can't prove it, but I think it is also pretty much true that the change innovations that have been created have tended not to continue to produce positive results for the organization for much beyond a year or two of their introduction. As is well-known, new senior management often discontinues some innovation that was put in with the help of a change consultant, and sometimes has fired all of the internal change agents as well. Changes that work well in one part of an organization are often not transferred to other parts. In general, there are few if any organizations of which it can be said that they are regularly and routinely managing themselves in their changing environments with a conscious, systematic approach to change. Yes, there are many intriguing initiatives, but few that stay the course for very long.

Why might this be? I think the present authors might argue, and if they did I would agree, that without a theory or model of the organization that is adequate to the situation the organization is in, planned change is always going to be a kind of random jabbing at the system. Research will tend not to evolve beyond interesting case studies to a body of knowledge about organization changing. Change projects will indeed fade away if organization members have not learned to think fundamentally differently about their system as *part of the change*—because learning to think fundamentally differently about the system is what the present times call for. Years ago, my colleague Jerry Harvey used to say, "The theory *is* the intervention." If theory is ad hoc and intuitive, it is not surprising that deeper, more sustained change does not occur.

These are the times of paradigm shift. But as Thomas Kuhn says somewhere, you often don't know the paradigm has shifted until well after people have begun to do their work and conduct their inquiries on the new basis. The old models are too deeply engraved in people's thinking. It takes time to understand at a conceptual level the kinds of intuitive insights change consultants have been having for the last couple of decades.

Olson and Eoyang are among the first to apply the principles of complexity science directly to the kinds of problems and situations that the OD field has always been concerned with. Over the past decade and a half, there have been several books about chaos and complexity science; these are discussed by the authors and listed in their bibliography. But until now, there has not been much work at the concrete level of how one is actually going to work with a client organization using ideas about "complex adaptive systems" as a base. That is what this book does, and as such, it really launches a new era in the field of planned organization change.

It is interesting to me that the authors manage to write their entire book without needing to dwell at great length on the interpersonal skills that are required of the consultant. The history of the OD field, of course, is replete with detailed discussions about the consultant's interpersonal skills, and a full measure of these abilities would be on anyone's list of requisite competencies. Olson and Eoyang clearly consider these competencies important, but they almost take it for granted that a consultant will possess these abilities to a high degree. The authors are really after another dimension of the consultant's behavior—the individual's frame or theory or conceptual basis for thinking the organization can change at all.

In the more traditional model, the possibility of change at all was not thought to rest on whether one understood the organization in the first place. Instead, it was assumed the organization was understood, but that the human relationships within this essentially pyramidal structure had to be improved. The way this would occur was through training and coaching in interpersonal skills, and by learning relatively simple psychological theories such as those of Maslow, Herzberg, and Rogers. Individual managers would learn to stop creating negative feelings in their associates, would learn to stop violating principles of good communication, would learn to stop assuming that people had to be told exactly what to do and. . .the organization would change. This approach—a bit simplified admittedly—didn't really presume *organization* development at all! It presumed development of human relationships within the organization.

It seems to me that it has become clearer and clearer in the past two decades that "organizations" are not the Tinker-Toy,® pyramidal structures that are so deep in our cultural psyche. "Organizations" might be modeled under some conditions as simple pyramids, but for at least thirty years the actual, concrete entities called "organizations" have found they could not do what needed to be done in that mode. So all kinds of informal structures and processes and channels and practices have had to be invented in order for work to get done, for requisite communications to occur, and for high quality human attitudes and actions to emerge.

"Complex adaptive systems" (CAS) theory is a new vessel, so to speak, that renders visible, legitimate, and significant a great deal more live human behavior than the older bureaucratic structures can countenance. A CAS is an entity that is going to change! It is going to evolve, adapt, develop, and exhibit extraordinary ingenuity in the process. All kinds of forms of human energy that are invisible and often taboo in the older structures are going to be present and available for engagement continually. Complex adaptive systems ideas are ways of talking about human systems that don't presume a lot of heavy-handed "leadership" and "management." Complex adaptive systems aren't on automatic pilot, of course; human judgment, creativity, and passion are as present as ever. But they are present as *part of the system*, woven into its essence, rather than as some add-on supplied by a "transformational leader" at the top, or an inspirational guru-consultant from the outside. For consultants, by the way, this means a more profound relationship to the system than older models that pretty much had the consultant as a detached free agent.

Olson and Eoyang are trying to help us look at the basic stuff of a human organization differently—especially a human organization in a turbulent and rapidly evolving environment. They draw their ideas from many sources, including, as I said above, the history of OD itself. But they also are out to introduce some ideas from chaos theory and complexity science that have never been an explicit part of the OD field.

Interestingly enough, one of the most powerful elements of the OD tradition—the so-called T-group or sensitivity training group—is not nearly as well-explained by OD's own traditional theories as by complex adaptive system theory! Amazingly, OD has as powerful a demonstration of the efficacy of CAS theories as it could possibly want right on its own professional doorstep! Using the author's three fundamental characteristics of self-organizing processes, we can say that a T-group is (1) a very special kind of "container" in time and space that needs to be very carefully created and sustained; within which (2) the true individual "differences" that make each human being special and unique can blossom alongside each other and energize each other, without any pressure to homogenize into each other; and that this occurs because of (3) a series of "transformational exchanges" that tend not to occur in a sustained, group-level way anywhere else. The result of the ongoing operation of these three characteristics is a guaranteed, but impossible to predict, self-organization of this type of grouping wherein no two are alike, yet all are interesting, memorable, and life-changing. Significantly, anyone experienced with these groups will say that if you want to guarantee *failure* in one of these settings, you will try to manage and control it. You have to "trust the process." As I have noted elsewhere,[3] it is unfortunate that the OD field never asked *why* we can trust the process, and instead left it as a rule of thumb. Complex adaptive systems theory explains why we *can* trust the process. Even more importantly, the authors show how we can trust the process of self-organizing on a much wider variety of organization problems. An organization does not have to be a T-group for there to be processes to trust, but we do have to learn how to think about a complex adaptive system in order to perceive what these processes are. This kind of learning I consider to be this book's most important contribution.

As a final observation, I would like to mention a personal significance for me of the authors' work. As some readers know, I have for some years myself been writing and speaking about rapid, chaotic change, under the rubric of "permanent white water." I have developed many vivid examples of these conditions in organizations

---

[3]Peter Vaill, "Integrating the Diverse Directions of the Behavioral Sciences." In Robert Tannenbaum, et al., *Human Systems Development*. San Francisco: Jossey-Bass, 1985, p. 562.

and their environments. I define "permanent white water" as a continual succession of *surprising, novel, ill-structured, and messy events,* which *force themselves on a manager's attention* and which, as an ongoing kind of disruptive event, *cannot be planned out of existence.* As I like to say, we're never going to get back to paddling our canoes on calm still lakes (read "orderly organization structures"), where we can pretty much go where we want to go, when and how we want to do so.

But there has always been a problem with the concept—at least until my exposure to complex adaptive systems thinking. How does anything get done in permanent white water? That's the problem. How do we still work productively in the midst of the swirl? What happens to the setting and pursuit of objectives? What becomes of acting intelligently in the midst of so much paradox and contradiction? What are the managerial and organizational equivalents of shooting an endless string of class 5 rapids, of making it through more or less in one piece and having some fun in the process? How are we to think of "leadership" in such contexts?

I have had a few ad hoc ideas, as has the OD field I've been a part of, band-aiding some concepts and rules of thumb because I didn't know how else to proceed. But I have never been satisfied with my ability to talk about taking action in permanent white water. Olson and Eoyang by no means have provided me with a complete recipe for action in complex adaptive systems, but the many ideas they do share in this book derive from a more consistent frame than I have found before, a frame moreover that is itself the object of much creative reflection and research, which means it will become richer and more powerful in the months and years to come.

This book is a kind of conceptual call to arms for thinking about organization change. Quite properly it is full of specific "best practices" in complex adaptive systems that managers and consultants can use to do what the authors advocate. But even more importantly in my view, Olson and Eoyang introduce us to some new "best theories" that are going to be shaping our thinking about human organizations for quite some time to come.

Peter Vaill
Minneapolis
June 2000

To Judith, who is my continual inspiration.
And
To John, who shares my emerging past, present, and future.

Preface

What's New?

Over the last ten years, we have witnessed a transformation in the business environment and echoing changes in mission, structure, resource allocation, change intervention strategies, and human interactions in organizations. These changes are not restricted to one locale or industry. They affect all stakeholders in all industries in all parts of the world. Some of these changes can be understood merely as exaggerations of or logical developments from the environments of the past. Others, however, seem to change the very nature of organizations and the interactions of humans in the corporate context. Some of the most obvious changes include:

- Globalization,
- High-speed communications,
- Emerging markets for goods and services,
- Technical innovations in products and services,
- Increased diversity of the workforce,

- Distribution of decision-making power across the organization,
- Reduced regulation and increased competition,
- Corporate mergers and acquisitions, and
- Customer demands for increased speed and quality at reduced prices.

All of these developments point toward the need for more flexible and adaptable organizational roles, responsibilities, and structures. Organizations must be able to recognize environmental changes, re-engineer themselves on the spot, and respond with products and services that fit the demands of the marketplace.

Impact on Organization Change

This environment of hyper-change puts tremendous demands on those who wish to facilitate organization change. Some expert change agents have developed solid intuitions, tools, and techniques that help build adaptability and flexibility. Individually and in small communities of practice, the profession has found ways to support fast-paced organization change. For the most part, however, change agents continue to struggle with outmoded models, tools, and techniques—ones that were sufficient in slower and simpler times, but that are counterproductive when complex adaptation is the only viable survival strategy. Sometimes, change interventions go as planned, and everyone is satisfied with the results. In many cases, however, things go awry. Disappointment and blame are broadly distributed.

Complex Adaptive Systems (CAS)

The science of *complex adaptive systems* provides an alternative to traditional models of organization change. Complexity science is an emerging theory that has implications for physics, biology, meteorology, and economics. It also provides a comprehensive and integrated explanation of how complex organizational systems adapt to uncertain environments.

According to Dooley (1996), "A complex adaptive system (CAS) behaves/evolves according to three key principles: (1) order is emergent as opposed to hierarchical; (2) the system's history is irreversible; and (3) the system's future is often unpredictable. The basic building blocks of the CAS are agents. Agents are semi-autonomous units that seek to maximize some measure of goodness or fitness by evolving over time."

To learn more about the science and mathematics of chaos and complexity, read *The Turbulent Mirror: An Illustrated Guide to Chaos Theory and the Science of Wholeness* by John Briggs and F. David Peat. They provide a fascinating look into the complex behaviors of nature that provide the metaphors for organization change addressed in this book.

Rather than focusing at the macro "strategic" level of the organizational system, complexity theory suggests that the most powerful processes of change occur at the micro level, where relationships, interactions, small experiments, and simple rules shape emerging patterns. Everything in an organization is interconnected, so large-scale change occurs through an integration of changes that affect the smallest parts. Organization change emerges from evolution of individuals and small groups. Like biological evolution, these changes are not always incremental. Sometimes a system will shift dramatically from one pattern to another in the course of its evolution (Gersick, 1991).

From a complexity perspective, everyone can be intentional change agents in an organization if they become more aware of options to help an organization adapt to its environment.

Complexity Theory and Organization

With the increasing influence of the Internet, networking, and partnerships on all organizations, the landscape of organic system changes is changing rapidly. This explains business's recent interest in complexity theory. It explains why change agents have to stay abreast of developments—or even leap ahead of them.

The escalating interest in complexity science in business is reflected in several recent publications, listed below:

- Clippinger (1999), *The Biology of Business*: Applies CAS principles to business issues of knowledge management, brand creation, market development, and organization change.

- Kelly & Allison (1999), *The Complexity Advantage*: Applies complexity theory to business practices.

- Lewin & Regine (2000), *Soul at Work*: Discusses patterns of behavior in case studies of complex adaptive systems.

- Lissack and Roos (1999), *The Next Common Sense*: Offers ten principles for aligning context, viewpoint, purpose, and action from complexity perspective.

- Petzinger (1999), *The New Pioneers*: Presents case studies of transformation of command and control hierarchies in U.S. businesses.

- Zimmerman, Lindberg, and Plsek (1998), *Edgeware*: Provides a resource guide to applications of complexity science for health care leaders.

Change Agent Perspective

The authors of this book consider applications of complexity from a change agent's perspective. Today, people holding various positions may take on the role of change agent: Internal and external consultants, senior executives, mid-to-upper-level managers, supervisors, front-line personnel, human resource officers, diversity consultants and trainers, community organizers, academicians, and students of organization change. All of these people will find this book helpful.

Every member of the organization has the potential to contribute to organization change, so each has something to learn from these pages.

Our own experience with clients demonstrates that complexity science reveals a world that is both patterned and surprising, both ordered and random. For OD consultants who traditionally have dealt with the human side of the enterprise, complexity science is a good match because it underscores the importance of relationships. Organization development consultants already know that the level of trust, caring, and connectivity affect the culture, productivity, and quality of the organizational outputs.

For change agents who rely on systems theory, complexity theory adds the perspective that organizations continuously evolve as they adapt to interactions with other systems and to the interaction of their subsystems.

A Jazzy Metaphor

Complexity provides a new lens through which to view the operation of the natural world. Applied to human systems, its metaphors and stories explain how people behave in groups and organizations. For example, a jazz ensemble is a complex mix of interactions among the individual musicians, their instruments, and the audience. They model a complex system that is continually adapting. We can look at the operation of a jazz ensemble and see the major concepts contained in this book.

Each of the musicians in a jazz ensemble is autonomous. They interact as they play. No formal conductor is needed. They bring their own intents, biases, levels of interest, experience, and aesthetics.

The minimum specifications of place, time, duration, melodies, roles, and general rules have been set. Usually the musicians know one another very well, and they are steeped in the theory and practice of jazz music. Frequently they have played the same or similar pieces before. The music is a balance of control and improvisation (the melodic and harmonic lines of in-the-moment changes and adaptations).

They listen to each other and adapt themselves to fashion the music. Each member's enthusiastic participation influences other members of the ensemble and the receptivity of the audience. The audience, in turn, influences the players with verbal and nonverbal expressions of appreciation.

The quality and creativity of the performance depends on all of these complex interactions. Emerging patterns, in turn, affect the performance on the next and successive pieces. Each performance is unique, but patterns are apparent.

The jazz ensemble metaphor indicates how creativity and efficiency emerge naturally within organizations. Change does not have to be imposed by managers or change agents. Some basic rules, positive contacts, and relationships among members of the organization allow solutions to emerge from the bottom up.

The individual musicians and audience members all function as autonomous *system agents*; the setting, the roles, the simple rules, and the duration of the session constitute the *container*; the contribution of each different instrument and the continuous change of melodies and harmony are *significant differences*. The influencing processes between the musicians and with the audience are *transforming exchanges*.

The continuous successions of music are the self-organizing *patterns* that emerge from the interactions.

In the following chapters the concepts italicized in the preceding paragraph will be expanded and related to the phenomenon of organization change.

Concepts presented in these chapters are highly interdependent, which is consistent with the themes of complexity. We recommend that the chapters be read in order because the new concepts are defined and examples are given when they first appear in the book. Each chapter presents tools and approaches to help change agents apply the principles of complexity to their work, including:

- Stories from our experience and others' to demonstrate how the principles of complexity and self-organizing systems help organizations be more adaptive and efficient;

- Case studies that show the ideas in action;

- Methods, including instructions, tools, and examples, to provide ideas for specific interventions and techniques; and

- Implications for the role of the change agent at each phase of work (contracting, assessing, intervening, and evaluating) defining how to focus on the system issues, actions that are appropriate, and outcomes to be expected.

How the Book Is Organized

In Chapter 1, An Emerging Paradigm of Organization Change, a new paradigm of self-organization is introduced and contrasted to the traditional organizational change models that promote prediction and control. The method, "Self-Organizing Dynamics," helps assess where an organization is in its self-organizing process.

Chapter 2, Change Through Connections, explores the transforming exchanges among system agents as the source of widely distributed leadership and organization change. Interventions for change must focus on massively entangled interactions of these agents that are going in many directions at the same time. This is contrasted with change controlled by leaders in a top-down process. The method, "Feedback Analysis," gives a framework for assessing and improving current feedback loops. The method, "Leader As Change Agent," suggests how leaders can most effectively influence change.

Chapter 3, Adapt to Uncertainty, explores the flexibility and adaptability of a healthy CAS and explains the importance of balancing predictability and surprise in an organization. This is contrasted with common assumptions that organization change follows predictable stages of development. The method, "Decision Making Under Conditions of Uncertainty," is useful for matching organization issues with appropriate decision-making methods.

Chapter 4, Emerging Goals, Plans, and Structures, describes the importance of emergence, action, and experimentation. This is contrasted with traditional practices of planning and organizing. The method, "Self-Organizing Exercise," helps a group experience self-organization.

Chapter 5, Amplify Difference, explores how differences are the engines for change in a complex adaptive system. The method, "Difference Matrix," helps a group see the value of dealing with significant differences and the consequences of ignoring them.

Chapter 6, Self-Similarity, describes how patterns that appear at one place are likely to appear elsewhere, giving meaning and binding the system together. The method, "Fractal As Metaphor," helps a group see similar patterns of behavior across the system.

Chapter 7, Success As Fit with the Environment, explains how efforts to adapt to the environment and to increase fitness involve balancing cooperation and competition and finding niches. This is contrasted with change initiatives that posit an ideal and work to close the gap with reality. The method, "Same and Different," helps a change agent to check the fit between different parts of the complex adaptive system (CAS).

Chapter 8, Self-Organization and the Change Agent, explores how the emerging paradigm of a CAS affects the role of an organization change agent, building requisite skills to function in a CAS, and presenting tips for thriving in the new paradigm. The method, "Reflection Evaluation," is useful for individual and group learning about the impact of their actions.

Chapter 9, Making Self-Organization a Reality, examines the future of organization change from a complexity perspective and summarizes essential perspectives and activities for working effectively as a change agent in a complex adaptive system (CAS). The chapter ends with an invitation to the reader to be involved in further exploration in facilitating organization change from a complexity science perspective by participating in our website, *www.complexod.com* (available March 1, 2001).

On Encountering a New Paradigm

Most organization change agents are aware of the concept of paradigm shifts. Most have probably helped clients cope with significant paradigm shifts in their industries. Most have also heard and read about organizational examples of persons who were slow to make a paradigm shift—the Swiss watch manufacturers (quartz movement), IBM (personal computers), Kodak (photocopiers), and so on.

We remind the reader that it is not just the "other people" who have difficulty in shifting paradigms. Because complexity theory is describing the same phenomena as do traditional approaches, it is sometimes difficult to distinguish between the old and the new. A common response is "What's new?" or "So what?" Certainly, aspects of complex adaptive systems (CAS) are consistent with what competent OD change agents do, such as facilitating large-system interventions (Bunker & Alban, 1997), but there are profound implications of the new paradigm for the change agent.

In their efforts to understand CAS, readers should view complexity concepts as a new lens that provides a clearer or broader view of what is happening in organizations. The basic principles are the same for individuals, teams, groups, corporations, and industries. The same patterns of emergence affect creativity, productivity, communications, teamwork, leadership, and many other organization activities that have, in the past, required different explanatory models. Complexity can provide an integrated and consistent means to understand a wide range of organizational phenomena. This integrated understanding can lead the change agent to new and innovative ideas for entering, assessing, intervening in, and evaluating organization change.

Acknowledgments

① WOULD LIKE TO ACKNOWLEDGE my early mentors in OD, including Howard Lamb, Don Klein, Dale Lake, Clayton Alderfer, Alan Drexler, Rad Wilson, Barbara Brewer, Susan and Tom Isgar, Peter Vaill, and Steve Ruma. I am grateful to the late Michael Merrill, Peter Mudd, and Fred Nader for sparking my interest in such things as fractals by co-sponsoring a conference with me in 1990 on OD, Jungian psychology, and chaos. My interest in complexity sciences and their application in OD was reawakened by a presentation by Mark Michaels at the 1998 ODN conference in New Orleans. He talked of his difficult ten-year effort to introduce the field of OD to the emerging paradigm of complexity science. I mentioned my interests in complexity science to Peter Vaill, who had talked about similar phenomena in the mid-1980s as "listening to weak signals." He suggested I contact Glenda Eoyang. Our subsequent collaboration is an example of how a small event can have large and unexpected outcomes.

In writing the book I have appreciated the helpful comments on early drafts by Bill Rothwell, Kristine Quade, Roland Sullivan, Lee Butler, Argentine Saunders Craig,

Denny Gallagher, David Schwandt, Charles Seashore, Kathy Hykes, Benton Randolph, Jo Cook, and Susan Rachmeler at Jossey-Bass/Pfeiffer. My son Eric, a science educator, helped clarify the use of natural science concepts in organizations. My co-author Glenda Eoyang developed the complexity model we use in this book. She has pioneered the application of complexity science to intractable problems in organizations. Working with her has been a delightful learning experience.

My family has been very encouraging and patient during this work. I regularly learn about the dynamics of self-organizing systems from the interactions of my children James, Eric, Loren, and Amy; from my daughters-in-law Lynn Patricia, Lynn Maria, and Dinah; from my son-in-law Shane; and from my grandchildren, Preston, Arne, and Arlo. My partner Judith, a facilitator of change in large systems, has provided valuable critiques along with loving support. I gratefully dedicate this book to her.

Ed Olson

I am pleased to have this opportunity to thank the teachers, students, and friends who have contributed to the personal and professional journey leading to this work.

Two institutions have influenced my choices about what and how to speak about complexity and human systems. St. John's College in Santa Fe, New Mexico, and Annapolis, Maryland, gave me a love for natural philosophy and a passion for learning in community. The Complexity Consortium, a group of professionals who reflect on their work as facilitators of change in complex systems, has helped me articulate and experiment with the ideas presented here.

Through countless conversations, colleagues and friends have demonstrated their patience with me and their passion for complexity. Special thanks go to Elaine Frankowski, Chris Nelson, Jeffrey Goldstein, Curt Lindberg, Kevin Dooley, Lois Yellowthunder, Vic Ward, Sally Dunn, Barbara Lauer, and Don Klein. My mother, Ruth Holladay, and my three sisters have made teaching and learning an integral part of life.

Client organizations have provided laboratories for expanding and testing the emerging concepts that are presented here. They deserve special thanks for their courage and curiosity.

Thanks to my co-author, Ed Olson, for his experience in OD and his tireless commitment to clarity and relevance, and to Peter Vaill, who recognized the potential of our partnership.

Finally, to my dear husband John, whose brilliance and courage have enriched my life beyond knowing. I cannot express enough thanks.

Glenda Eoyang

Self-Diagnosis

READERS MAY WISH TO COMPLETE the following diagnostic questionnaire before reading the book to gauge how closely their current system change practices match a complex adaptive perspective.

Organization Change Framework*

Instructions: Select the one or two best answers to each question below. If all choices are equally appealing, leave the item blank. Darken the circle(s) to indicate which answer(s) you chose. When you complete all questions, count the number of a's, b's, c's, d's you selected. Record the numbers in the "totals" boxes at the end of each page. Then add all together and complete the Profile on page xlvi.

	a	b	c	d
1. When I contract with a new client, I:	○	○	○	○
a) Guarantee specific outcomes.				
b) Shape client's expectations for outcomes.				
c) Indicate what I expect as outcomes.				
d) Acknowledge that the outcomes will emerge over the span of the project.				
2. When I begin a project, I:	○	○	○	○
a) Follow a clear step-by-step process.				
b) Begin with a clear plan, but am willing to change over time.				
c) Begin with a plan, but expect to change over time.				
d) Plan a first step and plan subsequent steps as I collect more information.				
3. My intervention processes and procedures:	○	○	○	○
a) Never vary.				
b) Are standard, but I make customized changes.				
c) Usually follow similar patterns.				
d) Are designed to meet the unique needs of each client.				
4. I believe that I can predict the reaction of a client organization:	○	○	○	○
a) All the time.				
b) Most of the time.				
c) Sometimes.				
d) Never.				

	a	b	c	d
TOTALS				

---

	a	b	c	d

5. When I plan an intervention, I collect information from: ○ ○ ○ ○
   a) Top management.
   b) All management.
   c) Key personnel in selected departments.
   d) All levels across the organization.

6. Individuals in the organization should be valued for: ○ ○ ○ ○
   a) Compliance with rules.
   b) Honesty about sources of success and failure.
   c) Increasing their level of competence.
   d) Creating patterns.

7. I prefer to begin my interventions: ○ ○ ○ ○
   a) At the top of the organization.
   b) With a key decision maker.
   c) Where there is the most need for change.
   d) At any organizational level with any group.

8. A team is empowered by: ○ ○ ○ ○
   a) A strong leader.
   b) Member interactions.
   c) Alliances with others.
   d) Autonomous individuals.

9. In effective organizations, decisions are based on: ○ ○ ○ ○
   a) Individual preferences.
   b) Team/unit consensus.
   c) Team/unit rules.
   d) Cumulative experience of individuals.

10. As a facilitator of change in an organization, I: ○ ○ ○ ○
    a) Give expert advice on organizational change.
    b) Hold a mirror up to the organization.
    c) Share insights about the organization's patterns of behavior.
    d) Learn and teach.

	a	b	c	d
TOTALS				

	a	b	c	d
11. An effective change facilitator should be able to:	○	○	○	○

    a) Squeeze ambiguity out of a system.

    b) Explain why there is ambiguity in the system.

    c) Help people feel comfortable in ambiguous situations.

    d) Use uncertainty and ambiguity to increase organizational capacity.

	a	b	c	d
12. I collect information about the success of an intervention:	○	○	○	○

    a) Only if the customer insists on it.

    b) At the end to provide a final report for the client.

    c) At the beginning, middle, and end.

    d) During every interaction with the organization.

	a	b	c	d
13. When I observe an organization, I look for:	○	○	○	○

    a) Roles that individuals play.

    b) Power relationships.

    c) Personal interactions.

    d) Patterns of behavior across the organization.

	a	b	c	d
14. A major factor in increasing the speed of change in an organization is:	○	○	○	○

    a) Competitive energy.

    b) Collaboration.

    c) Mutual respect and trust.

    d) Learning about the process of change.

	a	b	c	d
15. When you are facilitating organization change, you should begin with:	○	○	○	○

    a) The task that is most critical to the top managers.

    b) The simplest issues, so the group will build confidence over time.

    c) Actions most likely to succeed.

    d) The issues that are most accessible.

	a	b	c	d
TOTALS				

	a	b	c	d
16. Organization history is important because:	○	○	○	○

16. Organization history is important because:
   a) It predicts the future.
   b) It gives information about potential resistance.
   c) It provides stories to use in encouraging change.
   d) It builds the capacity for future action.

17. Differences in an organization: ○ ○ ○ ○
   a) Distract from the focus of the work.
   b) Provide variety in problem identification and solving processes.
   c) Keep people engaged and interested.
   d) Provide the impetus for transformation.

18. A highly functioning organization: ○ ○ ○ ○
   a) Meets a set of pre-defined criteria.
   b) Reflects the vision of its CEO.
   c) Satisfies the needs of all of its internal and external stakeholders.
   d) Fits into the niche formed by customers, competitors, and resources.

19. Change in an organization is like: ○ ○ ○ ○
   a) Tuning a machine.
   b) Freezing and unfreezing.
   c) Growth through developmental stages.
   d) Perpetual evolution.

20. I am a successful facilitator of change because I: ○ ○ ○ ○
   a) Know what will happen before it happens.
   b) Provide processes that are predictable.
   c) Am flexible in the face of adversity.
   d) Work with the patterns in the system.

	a	b	c	d
TOTALS				
GRAND TOTALS				

Profile

Scoring Instructions: In the table below, circle the number of responses you have in each category. Darken the space beneath the level you marked. The columns that result are the profile of your Organization Change Framework.

a	b	c	d
20	20	20	20
19	19	19	19
18	18	18	18
17	17	17	17
16	16	16	16
15	15	15	15
14	14	14	14
13	13	13	13
12	12	12	12
11	11	11	11
10	10	10	10
9	9	9	9
8	8	8	8
7	7	7	7
6	6	6	6
5	5	5	5
4	4	4	4
3	3	3	3
2	2	2	2
1	1	1	1
0	0	0	0

| Traditional change facilitation perspective | | | Complex adaptive system change perspective |

←───→

Interpretation

There is no "best" profile. The approach of a change agent must fit the expectations and needs of the client systems. The behavior listed in any of the alternatives, "a" through "d," may be appropriate, depending on the situation.

If your scores in the "a" and/or "b" columns are higher than your scores in the "c" and "d" columns, you may approach your work with a belief that organization change is best accomplished by clear, predictable means, using influence and position power to make change happen. This may be very appropriate if control is needed to capitalize on what is working well in a particular situation.

Columns "c" and "d" represent a complex adaptive perspective about organization change. This perspective is important for an organizational unit when it needs to be flexible and creative. A score of 20 in Column "d" represents a perspective that all aspects of organization change involve complex adaptive behavior. However, a high score in Column "d" may not equate to conscious expertise in complexity.

After reading and applying some of the concepts and methods in this book, retake the Organization Change Framework to see whether and how your scores change.

An Emerging Paradigm of Organization Change

THIS CHAPTER CONTRASTS the fundamental assumptions of the traditional paradigm of organization change with the paradigm that is emerging from the science of complex adaptive systems (CAS) (see Table 1.1). Problems with the old approaches are described in both theory and practice. A new complex model of self-organization is described and applied to organization change efforts.

Table 1.1. Traditional and CAS Models of Organization Change

Traditional Model of Organization Change	Complex Adaptive Model of Organization Change
Few variables determine outcomes.	Innumerable variables determine outcomes.
The whole is equal to sum of the parts (reductionist).	The whole is different from the sum of the parts (holistic).
Direction is determined by design and the power of a few leaders.	Direction is determined by emergence and the participation of many people.

Table 1.1. Traditional and CAS Models of Organization Change, Cont'd

Traditional Model of Organization Change	Complex Adaptive Model of Organization Change
Individual or system behavior is knowable, predictable, and controllable.	Individual or system behavior is unknowable, unpredictable, and uncontrollable.
Causality is linear: Every effect can be traced to a specific cause.	Causality is mutual: Every cause is also an effect, and every effect is also a cause.
Relationships are directive.	Relationships are empowering.
All systems are essentially the same.	Each system is unique.
Efficiency and reliability are measures of value.	Responsiveness to the environment is the measure of value.
Decisions are based on facts and data.	Decisions are based on tensions and patterns.
Leaders are experts and authorities.	Leaders are facilitators and supporters.

Organization As Machine

Our traditional world view about organizations is derived from Newtonian physics. This view presents the world as stable, predictable, unaffected by observation, and having clearly discernible causes and effects. From this perspective the organization is like a machine: Its parts determine the whole, and the whole is best understood by analyzing its components. The machine model is evident in current organizations. It can be seen in mechanistic thinking, focus on organization structure, rigorous analysis and measurement, search for root causes, decreasing variation, statistical quality control, extensive instructions for workers, increased specialization, drive for efficiency, and centralized command and control. Sometimes these approaches work, and sometimes they do not. Petzinger (1999) notes that "even as it was toppled from unassailableness in science, Newtonian mechanics remained firmly lodged as the mental model of management, from the first stirrings of the industrial revolution right through the advent of modern-day MBA studies" (p.19).

When we are operating in the machine paradigm, overspecification of designs or plans seems natural. We need to think of everything and work things out to the finest detail because the machine cannot think for itself. When we design physical equipment or other mechanistic aspects of the organization, the Newtonian concepts are appropriate.

Newtonian management methods work when:

- Systems are closed;

- Change is slow;

- Interdependencies are low;

- Certainty is high; and

- Variability is low.

In fact, even artificial intelligence machines need very detailed and specific instructions to deal with all likely contingencies. Think of the amount of programming required for the chess machine that can beat chess masters. There are many day-to-day organizational procedures that must be executed in a precise fashion, with little room for creativity. Routine generation of paychecks is such a procedure, but even the pay system needs periodic rethinking.

Bureaucracies, like machines, work well when conditions remain internally and externally stable. But is this ever truly the situation? If so, how long has it been since organizations functioned in a stable environment?

Changing the Machine

The change methodologies developed in this traditional environment have been *rational, top-down, expert-driven, and planned* change processes. Sound a little mechanical? Some authors have challenged this rational and mechanistic view (Morgan, 1997; Quinn & Cameron, 1988; Weick, 1977) and identified the political, intuitive, random, and irrational variables that have an impact on organizations. Organization change programs, however, continue to operate with rational Newtonian engineering assumptions. The assumption is that senior managers with wisdom will provide the vision for programs that yield significant short-term performance. For example, Ghoshal and Bartlett (1995) praise architects and leaders of organization turnarounds. Hagel (1994) recommends a top-down organization design process.

Evidence that top management has the power to drive change efforts is thin, at best. Take one example: As many as three-fourths of change initiatives such as TQM or re-engineering fail (Cameron, 1997; Senge, Kleiner, Roberts, Ross, Roth, & Smith,

1999). Zohar (1997) claims that most change agents and consultants introduce a change vocabulary with words like restructuring, vision, leadership, and creativity, but that they work within the existing machine-like structures that have no capacity for fundamental transformation. The problem is in trying to change hierarchical, authoritarian organizations (machine model) by recourse to hierarchical authority.

Problem with Traditional Approaches

Traditional approaches to organization change work sometimes. Too frequently, however, they fall short. Table 1.1 lists many differences between complexity science and traditional assumptions. Three of the basic truisms in traditional theory are false in fast-changing systems of today and tomorrow.

Truism 1: Change Starts at the Top

Many organization change initiatives start at the top and deal strongly with any resistance from system agents that blocks progress. Common ways of responding to resistance include downsizing, restructuring, and re-engineering.

System Agents

System agents are the participants in the self-organizing process. They may be individuals, teams, factions, or formal organizational entities. The difference among them and the interactions between them determine the patterns that emerge from the self-organizing process.

Even when change agents tap into the best thinking and energy of the people in the system—from the CEO to the workers on the front lines—assessment of the problem and intervention reflect the same paradigm that generated the problems in the first place.

Change Agents

Change agents are system agents who consciously influence the self-organizing process toward new and more adaptable patterns of relationship and behavior. They may be external or internal consultants, formal or informal leaders, or individual contributors to the work of the system.

Traditional notions of change management are clearly leader-driven. They are based on the principle of continuous measurement and controlling feedback on the people, processes, and systems within the organization. Change management approaches exercise strong control from the top by constructing processes for achieving strategic objectives.

Change agents are currently expected to calm turbulence during the change effort, to clarify the direction the organization wants or needs to go, and (sometimes) to be the leader of a total system change. What is wrong with this picture? Nothing—if the organization is a machine that needs kicking, oiling, or replacing parts, including its equivalent of a heart. In a self-organizing system, the leader has an important role to play, but creative and long-lasting change depends on the work of many individuals at many different levels and places in the organization.

Truism 2: Efficiency Comes from Control

The traditional paradigm of organization change holds deep, largely unconscious assumptions and values about efficiency and control. These prejudices undermine organizational adaptability. For example, when individuals are divided into small departments, information from the market environment is so diffused that no one in the organization understands what the market is saying about the organization as a whole. If tasks are standardized into "best practices," routines develop that are grooved and inflexible (Anderson, 1999).

To deal with this lack of continuous adaptation, organizations engage in continuous change efforts. Attempts to spot and fix defects create new, unanticipated problems. Anderson says, "Change initiatives follow change initiatives, eventually leading to cynicism about change management in general. Reorganizations eliminate one set of issues only for another to occur" (1999, p. 114).

In operational areas there is pressure to enhance performance. Subsystems are added to go beyond current limits, to handle the new exceptions, to provide better service, or to otherwise maintain or enhance system reliability. The problem is that each new operating subsystem has its own policies and procedures, and the whole system rapidly becomes overloaded with layers of subsystems. Whatever creativity and energy existed in the original system (for example, Apple in the early garage days) are locked in by the structures that have been laid on top of them. Typically, the organization tries to stretch and change by massaging old models to fit the new situation, such as by repackaging an old product or old plans to fit changed markets or by applying strategies to large organizations that work in small organizations.

Sometimes approaches based on existing assumptions and systems are appropriate, and sometimes they are not. The complex adaptive systems perspective provides an alternative that allows the change agent and others in the system to examine long-held assumptions and to generate new and creative solutions.

Truism 3: Prediction Is Possible

Managers act as if an interaction in one place will have a predictable or replicable result in another. Rarely does reality match this expectation, but managers continue to act as if it does. They develop detailed strategic plans and linear models of improvement, take actions, and then study why results do not match expectations.

The wisdom of complexity recognizes that all the individuals and subsystems in an organization are linked into complicated dances of change. A small change in one part of the system ripples through the organization and can have tremendous unintended consequences far from the site of the intervention.

These truisms represent basic assumptions about organizations and the processes that encourage change. The complex, open systems of today's organizational environments frequently make these assumptions invalid. Change agents today need viable alternatives.

Alternatives to the Machine Model

Many alternative change methods are available for a change agent. Holman and Devane (1999) identify over fifteen group methods that can guide change in large and small organizations, both for profit and nonprofit. Some innovative organization change strategies focus on motivation (relationships and quality of work life) as a means to change. Others turn their attention to resources (such as data, people as assets, knowledge, and power) to implement change. For still others, structures (teams and minimal hierarchy) or ultimate goals (objectives, values, visions) move the organization toward greater adaptability.

This variety produces a kind of cacophony that defies integration and does not allow any one voice to stand out as a logical alternative to the traditional explanations.

Given the ambiguity and lack of coherent theory, it is no wonder that we revert easily to the machine model. At least the machine model provides an intelligible view of the world and sets solid ground for decision and action. Until we have an equally powerful underlying model for the new world view, we will continue to revert to machine-based explanations and actions. We need a simple, coherent alternative to the old machine model before we can work responsibly in the complex environments of today and tomorrow.

Toward an Integrated Framework

Without an integrating theoretical frame, it is virtually impossible for the practitioner, to say nothing of clients, to comprehend the depth and breadth of the shift from machine to complex adaptive systems (CAS) views.

The way change facilitators think about causes of change determines how they contract, assess, intervene, and evaluate during their interactions with client organizations. If they see causality in terms of traditional systems theory, then they look for systems archetypes (Senge, 1990). If they see causality as an equilibrium-seeking resolution of tension, they look for ways to unfreeze and refreeze (Lewin, 1951). If they see an organization as a machine, they re-engineer its functions or replace dysfunctional parts (Hammer & Champy, 1994). How does one conceptualize change in a complex adaptive system? What foundation does a new integrated framework provide for assessment, intervention, and evaluation of organization change efforts?

Complex Adaptive Systems

A *complex adaptive system (CAS)* behaves/evolves according to three key principles: (1) order is emergent as opposed to hierarchical, (2) the system's history is irreversible, and (3) the system's future is often unpredictable. The basic building blocks of the CAS are agents. Agents are semi-autonomous units that seek to maximize some measure of goodness or fitness by evolving over time (Dooley, 1996).

Recent discoveries in the physical sciences provide a rich source for innovative models for change in organizations. The "new sciences" of chaos, complex adaptive systems, nonlinear dynamics, and quantum theory all provide revolutionary ways of thinking about causality in natural systems. Various writers have taken these ideas and applied them to organization behavior and management approaches (Dooley, 1997; Eoyang, 1997; Goldstein, 1994; Guastello, 1995; Hurst, 1995; Kauffman, 1995; Kiel, 1994; Kelly, 1994; Kelly & Allison, 1998; Kelso, 1995; Stacey, 1992; Van de Ven & Garud, 1994; Waldrop, 1992; Wheatley, 1992; Youngblood, 1997; Zimmerman, Lindberg, & Plsek, 1998). The purpose of this book is to provide an integrated framework, examples, and tools to help change agents apply these concepts to their own organizational challenges.

By Any Other Name

The study of complexity draws from many different disciplines, each with its own language and special applications.

- Autopoiesis—biology;

- Complex adaptive systems—computer simulation modeling;

- Deterministic chaos—mathematics;

- Dissipative structures—thermodynamics;

- Emergence—biology and social sciences;

- Fractal geometry—mathematics;

- Nonlinear dynamics—engineering;

- Nonlinear time series analysis—engineering;

- Self-organized criticality—engineering and computer simulation models; and

- Self-organizing systems—biology and computer simulation modeling.

One underlying question shapes the application of complexity theory to organization development: Is a functioning organization really a complex adaptive system? Or does complex adaptive system theory simply provide a new way to think and talk about patterns of organization behavior? This subtle distinction may not matter to a pragmatic practitioner, who focuses on understanding for action. A change agent in the field can design interventions "as if" the system were complex adaptive and move toward productive outcomes. Most readers of this book are probably practitioners who work comfortably in the "as if" mode. For ease of description, this text presents complex adaptive systems as if they were real and distinct from noncomplex adaptive systems.

Pattern, in this context, refers to any coherent structure that emerges from a self-organizing process. Patterns are discernible when similarities and differences are repeated in identifiable sequences and relationships across a system. Examples include corporate culture, behavioral norms, use of jargon, modes of dress, habits of interaction, and so on.

For the theoretical and philosophically inclined, however, the question of reality or perception is an important one. Unfortunately, its resolution is beyond the scope of this book. Researchers in various fields are designing experiments to test the scientific reality of the theory. Philosophers are building arguments for and against the ontological reality of the theory of complex systems. Change agents can use those discoveries. The lessons from complexity can lead to understanding and informed action by change agents as they engage the real-world problems of their real-world clients.

Change in a Complex Adaptive System

We believe that change comes about in a cyclical fashion in a complex adaptive system. The dimensions of change in a CAS are illustrated in Figure 1.1, Self-Organizing Dynamics. This illustration presents an iterative process in two phases. The phases happen on many dimensions and at many different parts of the organization at the same time.

Figure 1.1.   Self-Organizing Dynamics

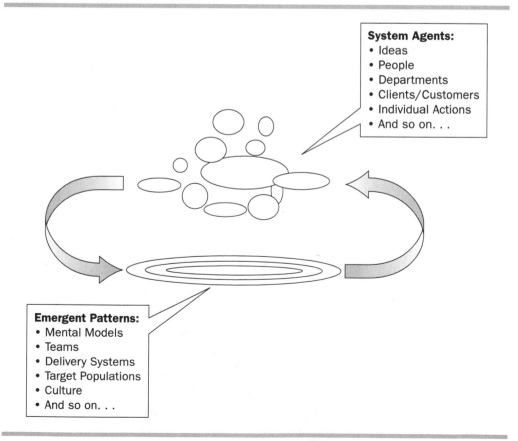

System Agents:
- Ideas
- People
- Departments
- Clients/Customers
- Individual Actions
- And so on. . .

Emergent Patterns:
- Mental Models
- Teams
- Delivery Systems
- Target Populations
- Culture
- And so on. . .

Self-organization is the tendency of an open system to generate new structures and patterns based on its own internal dynamics. Organization design is not imposed from above or outside; it emerges from the interactions of the agents in the system.

One phase starts with the parts of the system (system agents) and generates a whole, system-wide pattern. The other phase begins with the system-wide pattern (emergent patterns) and affects the interactions of the parts. Each phase is described in more detail below.

From the Part to the Whole

In this theory of change, parts of the system (agents of any size or structure) interact in real time. As they interact, patterns emerge from the system as a whole. The downward arrow on the left side of Figure 1.1 illustrates this phase. For example, a company's marketing and sales force over time develops a pattern for generating leads, strategies for contacting customers, and ways of relating with the production and accounting departments. These patterns are the result of many cycles of interaction. New salespeople are expected to learn the ropes. With the introduction of new technology such as a cell phone or new concepts like just-in-time manufacturing, the old patterns give way to new. The organization reinvents itself every day by making small adjustments in its patterns.

This phase is only part of the whole process, however. The whole also affects the parts.

From the Whole to the Part

At the same time that new patterns are emerging, the old patterns are influencing the behavior of the agents.

Corporate culture, group norms, and documented procedures are examples of ways in which previously emerged patterns become entrenched and affect available options for agents' later actions. Patterns of organizational interaction establish traditions and habits of organization life that tend to bring order.

On the one hand, this constraint is beneficial because it makes some actions and decisions automatic, releasing energy for more creative and challenging tasks. On the other hand, too much dependence on old patterns of behavior locks individuals and groups into habits that may not be adaptive in new circumstances. The upward arrow on the right side of Figure 1.1 denotes this phase of the process.

The system-wide patterns can be considered both effects (of previous agent interaction) and causes (of future agent behavior). As the patterns emerge, they constrain the behaviors of the parts in their future interactions. In this messy and iterative manner, the system lurches and searches its way to new organizational relationships and structures that integrate internal and external forces.

Emergent Patterns Through Self-Organization

The agents of a complex adaptive system interact, and patterns form over time. The patterns then affect how the parts interact to form future patterns. Change agents are well-aware of this cyclical process of interaction and group formation. Knowing that this evolutionary process takes place, however, does not necessarily provide the change agent with effective options for action.

Complex adaptive systems studies in both social and physical sciences, however, provide insight into the ways that the patterns emerge and provide guidance for the change agent who wishes to influence the evolution of new and innovative patterns. Complex adaptive systems investigations have revealed that three factors shape self-organizing patterns: container, significant difference, and transforming exchanges.[1]

By understanding and manipulating these three conditions, the change agent can support effective self-organization.

Conditions for Self-Organization

Three factors influence the placement, shape, and power of the patterns that emerge in complex adaptive systems: (1) container, (2) significant differences, and (3) transforming exchanges. These three conditions for self-organization are described in detail below.

Container

Container sets the bounds for the self-organizing system. It defines the "self" that organizes. The container may be physical (for example, geographic location), organizational (for example, department), or conceptual (for example, identity, purpose, or procedures).

---

[1]For a complete explanation of the sources, derivation, and testing of this approach to self-organizing human systems, refer to G.H. Eoyang, *Conditions for Self-Organization in Human Systems.* Unpublished doctoral dissertation, Union Institute, Cincinnati, OH, 2001.

A *container* establishes the semi-permeable boundary within which the change occurs. Within this container, new relationships and structures form over time. Many different aspects of a system can serve as a container. A physical container exists when the persons who work in the same building develop relationships that are different from those they have with persons who work in remote locations. An organization container exists when members of one department interact among themselves differently than they interact with others. Professional, personal, psychological, social, and cultural containers shape the behavior of people in every environment.

Examples of Containers

- *Physical* (building, campus);

- *Organization* (department, function);

- *Behavioral* (professional identification, culture); and

- *Conceptual* (purpose, procedures, rules, budgets).

Containers hold the parts of the system together so that the self-organizing process can move forward. This cohesive force can take a variety of forms. Sometimes the container is a central purpose or charismatic leader that pulls the parts of the system together. This type of container works like a *magnet* to draw agents into the system. In other situations, the container can function like a *fence*, defining the outside limit of the system. Physical boundaries or group membership criteria provide such fence-like containers for a system. A third type of container depends on the one-to-one connections among agents. Natural *affinities*, such as culture, gender, or personal history, bind the agents in a system together. The type of container (magnet, fence, or affinity) determines the shape and speed of the emerging patterns.

JUST AS A PERSON NEEDS time and space to incubate thoughts before a new idea can emerge, a system needs a bounded space for the emergence of new patterns.

Any one, or all, of these structures can provide the history, beliefs, values, or norms that constrain and contain the emerging patterns in the system. Thus contained, the interactions of the agents can have sufficient time and opportunity to make contact and allow the self-organizing changes to occur. Just as a person needs time and space to incubate thoughts before a new idea can emerge, a system needs a bounded space for the emergence of new patterns.

In a CAS, containers are not mutually exclusive. One individual can be "within" multiple containers at the same time, such as two sets of role expectations from two different bosses in a matrixed organization. He or she may experience dissonance, frustration, and confusion when trying to participate in two containers simultaneously, especially when the two are evolving toward quite different patterns of behavior.

A human system that is without a clear container risks dissolution. If a new Internet start-up company does not successfully develop a corporate identity to differentiate itself clearly from its competition, there will not be sufficient ground for self-organization.

Significant Differences

Significant differences determine the primary patterns that emerge during self-organizing processes. A difference between two agents may be reflected and reinforced by other agents in the system, which then establishes a system-wide pattern.

Any difference that exists in the system can serve as the difference that will shape the emergent patterns. The possibilities are endless because a CAS can have an unlimited number of differences.

Examples of Significant Differences

- Power;
- Levels of expertise;
- Quality;
- Cost;
- Gender;
- Race; and
- Educational background.

If, for example, level of expertise is a significant difference, the patterns that emerge will embody the various areas of knowledge and experience inherent among the agents. If gender is a significant difference, then sexual and social expectations will appear in the emerging patterns. Each significant difference will shape the emergent pattern differently.

The many differences in a system are important to various members of the group at the same time. Also, the differences change continuously as the concerns and needs of the group shift. A group that focuses myopically on a single difference increases its potential to act in consistent and coherent ways, but it also risks locking itself into a narrow range of responses. A group that cannot agree on a single focal difference, on the other hand, may generate a large number of possibilities, but be unable to gain the momentum necessary to take action on any one of them.

Transforming Exchanges

Transforming exchanges form the connections between system agents. Information, money, energy, or other resources are the media for transforming exchanges. As the resource flows from agent to agent, each is transformed in some way. These patterns of individual change lead, ultimately, to adaptability of the system as a whole.

Transforming exchanges are the third of the conditions that shape the emerging patterns in a complex system. "Exchanges" refers to the contact between agents of the self-organizing system. The agents may be members of the organization, ideas, departments, or customers. When one agent changes, it sends messages in the form of energy, information, or material to its neighbors. The neighboring agents receive the messages and respond to them in the local environment. That response generates more messages that are consumed and responded to by other agents.

Examples of Vehicles to Build Transforming Exchanges

- Face-to-face meetings;
- E-mail;
- Delivery of products and services;
- Financial transactions;
- Memos; and
- Phone calls.

Transforming exchanges, via any medium, connect across significant differences and create changes in the patterns around which the system organizes itself. When transforming exchanges are insufficient, agents work as disjointed and independent parts, and then coherent, system-wide patterns fail to emerge. Individual agents experience a sense of isolation and confusion. When transforming exchanges are too strong or too numerous, agents have few degrees of freedom and thus their behaviors are limited. For example, information overload or rigid management practices can produce groupthink and lack of creativity, direct results of immediate and tight transforming exchanges, which prohibit individual decisions by the agents.

Transforming exchanges occur naturally in human systems. Sometimes the natural ones are productive and sometimes not. A change agent can shape existing exchanges or design new ones to optimize the system's ability to transform itself and adapt to its environment. Chapter 2 includes *Method: Feedback Analysis,* which provides a detailed process a change agent can use to analyze and refine transforming exchanges in a system. *Coping with Chaos: Seven Simple Tools* (Eoyang, 1997) also provides tips for establishing effective transforming exchanges.

The Self-Organizing Process

When beginning an engagement with a new client, one of the first things a change agent notices are the clusters, groups, and subgroups that determine what work is done and how it is done. Managers at different organizational levels form active associations that support consistent behavior across the company. Functional divisions, such as research and development, manufacturing, and distribution, have their own internal structures for decision making and action. Informal groups of colleagues form because of shared interests or histories. Sometimes, groups are located at remote geographical sites, and the physical distances shape groups that behave more or less in concert. The organization itself becomes a container that distinguishes it from its customers and competitors. These naturally occurring systems and subsystems shape individual and group behaviors. Within a container, various perspectives are shared, and group identity emerges.

Within and between containers, significant differences shape behavior. In an effective project team, for example, different areas of expertise determine roles and responsibilities of members. Across an organization, differences in strategic importance of divisions may determine which management voices are more powerful. In times of change, differences in seniority may shape how individuals react. In each container, a unique set of significant differences determines the patterns of behavior for individuals and for the group as a whole. Other sets of differences may shape the emergent behavior between containers, affecting the patterns of behavior that emerge in larger organizational containers.

Difference alone does not generate change, however. Team members may be completely aware of their differences, but be unwilling to engage with one another to learn from their various perspectives. When this happens, the system becomes locked in to destructive behavior that exaggerates differences without using its potential for learning and growth. Within a container, the agents become aware of their differences and use transforming exchanges to engage other agents in the system. Such engagement among agents within a container generates new patterns of behavior, new ideas, new products, and innovative ideas for process improvement.

In a transforming exchange, one agent shares information with another. The second listens, learns, is transformed, and shares information back with the first. Over time, this exchange allows the two to build new insights and options that transcend the original differences between them. Through this process, the agents do not become identical to each other. Rather, each learns from the other and discovers new ways to use their differences toward common ends.

In the course of assessment, a change agent should become aware of the existing containers, their internal and external significant differences, and the habits of transforming exchange that have shaped behavior in the past. Based on this knowledge, the change agent can design interventions to shift container, difference, or exchange patterns to alter the path of self-organization in the group.

THE ROLE OF THE change agent is to use an understanding of the evolving patterns to shift the container, differences, or exchanges to affect the self-organizing path, to observe how the system responds, and to design the next intervention.

Although the interventions can be planned and consciously designed to shape self-organizing patterns, not even the most competent change agent can identify specific causes or predict specific outcomes of the actions of any agent in the system. The role of the change agent is to use an understanding of the evolving patterns to shift the container, differences, or exchanges to affect the self-organizing path, to observe how the system responds, and to design the next intervention. The objective of this action-oriented experimentation is to anticipate, adapt, and influence, not to predict or control the behavior of the system. Later chapters in this book describe specific methods for influencing these three conditions of self-organization.

No Condition Stands Alone

It is helpful to think about and work with these three conditions for self-organization as if they were distinct, but they are not. In the real system interactions, all three conditions are intimately linked together. A change in one shifts the behavior of the system, which results in changes in the other two conditions. For this reason, a change agent can introduce a single intervention that will have far-reaching effects across the system.

Change that took place in an international financial services organization will illustrate how the conditions are interconnected. Originally a North American company, the client had pursued an acquisition strategy to build an international presence. Over a period of three years, they purchased ten companies in Western Europe. Initially, the acquired companies were allowed to pursue their own strategic and tactical plans without much interference from the parent company. The challenge was to help integrate the various organizations into a single strategic unit. On the face of it, this integration process could be viewed as a container problem: Develop a single corporate identity to embrace the various entities.

Implementing this single identity, however, would give significance to a host of differences that had previously been irrelevant. Variations in language, computer systems, and corporate cultures would emerge within the new container.

Building and maintaining the integrated organization required new modes of communication to form transforming exchanges between and among the various parts of the organization. All three conditions—container, difference, and exchanges—were equally critical issues in shaping the self-organization of a productive whole.

One might think that such complicated interconnections would make the job of organization change more difficult, but in fact it simplifies the process. Change agents who are aware of self-organizing patterns recognize that an intervention that affects any of the conditions shifts the corporate dynamic and results in changes to the others. Given this picture of the self-organizing process, one intervention can be used to alter the most accessible of the conditions, with the recognition that the other conditions will be changed as a result.

In the example above, transforming exchanges were the easiest of the conditions to change. All of the corporate partners had cultures of face-to-face communication. Many of the staff and leaders were people-oriented extroverts. Recognizing this common strength, an intervention was designed to increase feedback among all employees. Using technology, the change agent established several online conversations to involve individuals from all of the companies in rich, work-related, problem-solving discussions. These interactions formed foundation on which corporate integration could be based. As individuals and groups across our sample company were connected, they began to identify and resolve their own significant differences and to think of themselves as part of the same, international, corporate entity.

CAS and the Change Agent

The self-organizing dynamic we presented in Figure 1.1 focuses on the containers that hold the system, the differences that focus pattern-forming energies of the system, and transforming exchanges that establish both stability and the potential for change at the individual and organization levels simultaneously. This iterative and adaptive model sets a new framework for a change agent's understanding and activities.

THE CHANGE AGENT can assess the current state of the containers, differences, and exchanges in an organization; select the one condition that is easiest to affect; make an intervention; and evaluate how the other conditions shift in the process of self-organization.

Because of the complex adaptive nature of the organization, all three of the self-organizing conditions depend on all of the others. No one is more causal to the process than any other. The change agent can assess the current state of the containers, differences, and exchanges in an organization; select the one condition that is easiest to affect; make an intervention; and evaluate how the other conditions shift in the process of self-organization. As the system adapts, the change agent repeats the process to assess, intervene, and evaluate. This experimental and iterative process is the most effective method for a change agent to influence the paths and products of self-organization in human systems.

The model of self-organizing dynamics (Figure 1.1) can be used as a template for an initial scan of an organization (see Method: Self-Organizing Dynamics, p. 20). This template shows how similar patterns appear across all parts of the organization and across all behavioral issues. This helps a client to focus his or her energy on small, immediate changes that can have a large impact.

The CAS framework also generates some assumptions and recommends some actions that directly contradict the wisdom of traditional change facilitation. Table 1.2 contrasts the traditional assumptions about change in organizations with the CAS assumptions that will be explored in the following six chapters.

Table 1.2. Assumptions About Change

Chapter	Traditional	Complex Adaptive Systems
2	Top down	Depends on connections between system agents
3	Groups follow predictable stages of development	System agents adapt to uncertainty
4	Clear goals and structures	Emerging goals, plans, and structures
5	Values consensus	Expects tension between self-similarity and difference
6	Levels of intervention (individual, group, organization)	Self-similarity across system
7	Defines success as closing the gap with a preferred future	Defines success as fit with environment

The rest of this book presents concepts, tools, and techniques to help change agents to work effectively in a CAS.

Summary

The use of rational planned change approaches, driven by leaders with the help of change facilitators, has fallen short even when bolstered by formal (and expensive) programs such as TQM and re-engineering. The root of the problem has been the Newtonian legacy of organization-as-machine.

A new paradigm is needed—one that creates the conditions for fostering information flow, connectivity, relationships, and the emergence of plans from the members of the organization. Such a paradigm has major implications for leaders and change agents. Learning to support these processes and letting go of the need for control and certainty is a major challenge. The building blocks of organizations of the future will be the new effective connections, actual and virtual.

The emerging science of complex adaptive systems offers such a paradigm. It provides metaphors and models that articulate and make meaning out of the emerging adaptive nature of organizations. It establishes a foundation for a new theory of change, which, in turn, offers multiple ways to assess an organization's current situation, intervene to influence, and evaluate outcomes of change initiatives. As a powerful theoretical model, CAS provides an integrating context for the many inno-vative tools and techniques that are emerging from the various corners of the change-facilitation field. It meets the need for a model that is simple and complex, adaptable and stable, optimal for individual and organization, ambiguous and articulate, diverse and integrated, revolutionary and strangely familiar.

▶ METHOD: SELF-ORGANIZING DYNAMICS

Purpose

The three conditions of self-organization can be used to provide an over-all assessment of where an organization is in its self-organizing process (see Exhibit 1.1).

Exhibit 1.1. Assessment of Needs for Self-Organization

Conditions for Self-Organization	Totally Constrained System	Self-Organizing System	Totally Unconstrained System
Container	Strong, Small	Permeable boundaries are good enough to let the system self-organize	Weak, Large
		←————————————→	
Significant Differences	Hidden or None Acknowledged	Differences that are constraining/ unconstraining the system are identified and worked through	Many or Every Difference Is Equally Acknowledged
		←————————————→	
Transforming Exchanges	Many, Top-Down Only, Tight Coupling	Meaningful contacts among agents forming the patterns in the system	Few, Trivial
		←————————————→	

Preparation

Existing data about the organization can be used for this method, or additional data can be collected through focus group interviews. In meetings with the client, the change agent helps the group organize the data into three categories corresponding to the three conditions for self-organization.

This method is consistent with the model developed by L. Dave Brown (1980). Brown pointed out that overconstrained organizations suppress crucial information, ignore differences, are bound by rules, constrict novelty, and are impermeable to novel inputs. An underconstrained organization is unfocused, unable to identify relevant information, withdrawn from conflict, inefficient, fragmented, and too permeable to disruptive inputs. When in either extreme state, the organization is not able to self-organize; it is either too tightly controlled or too loosely controlled.

Process

The client must determine whether the organization is overconstrained or underconstrained in each of the three conditions (see Exhibit 1.1).

If the organization is tipped toward being overconstrained, interventions to move it toward less constraint will support its movement to self-organization (represented by the center of each continuum). If the organization is underconstrained, it requires interventions to move it toward more constraint—and thus bring it into the realm of self-organization.

As the change initiative moves back and forth on each continuum, the system comes in and out of a state of self-organization. The ideal for a CAS is to match its self-organizing patterns to fit its environment. A nuclear power plant must be on the highly constrained end of the continuum, and day traders have to be at the underconstrained end because their environment is uncontrolled.

THE IDEAL for a CAS is to match its self-organizing patterns to fit its environment.

Application

The managers of a human resource department had received a low assessment in the annual employee survey and wished to improve their scores. They were under pressure from top management to take action. The consultant conducted focus group interviews and arranged the data in nine themes, which the management group classified in the categories representing the three conditions of self-organization (see Exhibit 1.2).

Exhibit 1.2. Sample Assessment of Needs for Self-Organization

Conditions for Self-Organization	Totally Constrained System	Self-Organizing System	Totally Unconstrained System
Container	Strong, Small		Weak, Large
1. Need for big picture		←————————●	
2. More focus on work		←————————●	
3. Clarify roles and expectations		←————————●	
Significant Differences	Hidden or None Acknowledged		Many or Every Difference Is Equally Acknowledged
4. Develop staff		←————————●	
5. Ensure equity in rewards		←————————●	
6. Hold people accountable		←————————●	
Transforming Exchanges	Many Top-Down Only, Tight Coupling		Few, Trivial
7. Seek out different ideas		←————————●	
8. Give timely and direct feedback		←————————●	
9. More direct communication from front office		←————————●	

The managers agreed that all of the indicators pointed toward the need to tighten up a diffuse underconstrained system. The containers were too large and diffuse for staff to know how management regarded their work. Management had also been ignoring significant differences among the staff over inequities in work assignments and performance. Management had also avoided transforming exchanges with the staff through direct contact. Management was seen as unengaged or uninterested in staff ideas.

With all of the pressures on the management group, they realized that they could not make progress in all areas at once. Knowing that the conditions of self-organization are interconnected, the management team decided to focus on one area, trusting that improvement in one of the staff concerns would favorably impact the others.

The leader of the group chose to improve transforming exchanges, particularly the quality of interaction with the staff. He committed to (1) engaging the staff on specifics of their projects, (2) clarifying how their activities contribute to the big picture, and (3) expressing his own vision of where the group was going. This would shrink the container by building a strong sense of being a team. The leader would address the significant differences in how staff members related to their tasks, and the direct contact with the staff would be a series of transformative exchanges, one-on-one and in small groups.

The management group identified some goals and actions to move them toward the work focus (see Exhibit 1.3).

Exhibit 1.3. Sample Goals and Actions

Goals	Actions
Develop more time to focus on the internal work	Delegate some external tasks to middle managers
Validate HR's vision about the work and build support	Talk to key internal customers
Enhance communications with staff about the work	Monthly meetings; spontaneous meetings; visit work groups
Clear, direct, timely action (from the heart)	Hire executive coach to help with communications
Obtain more suggestions from staff about the work	Set up feedback sessions with work groups

The management group committed to take these actions over a two-month period and to obtain regular feedback on the outcomes of their actions.

After two months the management reviewed the original nine areas of concern from the staff and refocused their change initiative. ◀

The model of self-organizing dynamics illustrates the value of complexity science for the organization change agent. By using the model to focus attention on increasing the capacity of the organization to self-organize, the change agent fosters the meaningful and adaptive interconnectedness of parts of the system. In the next chapter we see how improving connections among system agents leads to organization change.

②

Change Through Connections (Not Top-Down Control)

THE SYSTEM AGENTS in a self-organizing system are continually interacting in a variety of directions, all at the same time. They do not necessarily act in concert—or by consensus. Each stretches to interact with other parts of the organization in ways that make sense in the moment.

This chapter examines such complex interactions in organizations and points out ways that leaders and change agents can influence these interactions to promote change.

THE MAJOR BUSINESS of leadership is to engage with all system agents to foster their interconnectedness, not to try to control those interactions.

The major business of leadership is to engage with all system agents to foster their interconnectedness, not to try to control those interactions. If leaders were not formally designated, they would arise from the interactions. Leaders and change agents engage all system agents in the organization's specific and urgent business issues; they work across both hierarchy and function; and they encourage new patterns of interaction about innovation and accountability.

The following story about a hospital merger shows how interconnections of system agents can threaten the control mechanisms of leaders.

▶ STORY: HOSPITAL MERGER

A consultant team was hired to work with two health systems that had "merged." In reality the change was a "takeover," but that is getting ahead of the story.

"Regional Hospital," a respected community hospital, was purchased by "Vantage Hospital System." Both hospitals had strong and quite distinct cultures.

The new CEO of the merged hospitals was from "Regional." He urged the external consultants to propose a change process to support the organizational transformation. Based on a series of focus group meetings, the consultants developed a database about the two systems and met with a liaison group, including representatives from the two hospitals. The group developed a strategy to help all members of both systems explore and appreciate their cultural differences.

The interactions of the system agents supported the cultural integration by developing a high degree of connection, creativity, understanding, and trust within a short time. When the leaders of the "Vantage" system saw the results on a small scale, they realized they were losing control. If continued on a large scale, the system-wide conversations would block plans to impose procedures and values on the merged system.

As the liaison group highlighted the significant differences between the two hospitals, the chances for self-organization within the new merged system were increased. This threatened the Vantage leaders, who were unwilling to trust the outcome of the process. The leaders were unwilling to trust the dynamics of a CAS. They preferred to run their new system in a traditional, autocratic, top-down fashion, which had "worked" for many years. ◀

In this chapter we explore how leaders and change agents can influence the connections of system agents in a complex system without taking over control. Leadership that is widely distributed in a CAS is connected and engaged with many other agents in the system. Leaders see the potential of what can emerge and create a climate that helps members find meaning in their connections with one another. Change agents help both leaders and all system agents to learn about emerging patterns.

Entangled Connections

Interactions among system agents that are going on everywhere at the same time produce patterns of change. In a CAS the system is massively entangled, so one way to influence change is to influence the interaction.

In Figure 2.1 the directions of the small arrows show the various paths of the system agents as an unlimited number of possibilities. The change agent can have influence in the midst of these ongoing interactions. The actions include the whole range of change agent behavior: counseling a leader, asking process questions of a group, providing expert advice, or watching in silence.

> **CHANGE CANNOT BE a simple top-down process. It must work from every point in the system toward every other point.**

Figure 2.1. Massive Entanglements of Agents

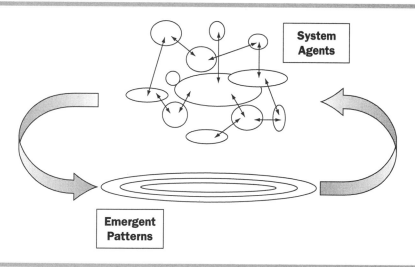

System Agents

Emergent Patterns

In a complex adaptive world, multiple interdependencies, causal connections, and the flow of power move every which way at the same time. Change cannot be a simple top-down process. It must work from every point in the system toward every other point.

With many containers for change and multiple fluid boundaries, the influences for change or stability can be found throughout the organizational structures. Most organizations are also finding that their longstanding relationships with customers, suppliers, regulators, and competition are also becoming massively entangled.

The boundaries between individuals, groups, and organizations are fuzzy and continually renegotiated. For example, consolidation of banking, insurance, and securities firms creates complicated relationships among products, services, and processes. When these organizations are international, the problems are magnified by exchange rates, cultural differences, and language.

Why are elements in a CAS massively entangled?

- Electronic communication

- Shifting product lines

- Connections with clients

- Personal/historical interactions

- Business interdependence

- Cross-functional teams

- Changing processes, roles, and responsibilities

- Fewer people to do more work

The traditional model of systems dynamics is sufficient for describing some system behaviors, but in some cases decisions made any place in the system may have serious, effects on other parts of the system. Decisions, information, and energy flow back and forth and up and down across the system. Influences for change or for stability can be found at any level. Decision makers must be sensitive to changes that may come from many different parts of the CAS.

The model of self-organization in Chapter 1 (shown in Figure 1.1) shows only one coupled set of agents and emergent patterns. In reality, many of these sets are working at the same time. They are distinguishable from each other, but they also influence each other. For example, a person is part of a work group, a van pool, a clique that eats lunch together, a professional organization, a faith community, a family, and a neighborhood. Through their memberships, all of these self-organizing groups are entangled with all of the others. Any one may affect the others. What happens in one container may have repercussions in any or all of the other emerging containers.

No Single Source of Change

Much of traditional language about change in organizations is borrowed from the world of Newtonian physics: for example, pressure, force, momentum, inertia, and resistance. Our traditional strategies, too, derive from an expectation of a single forceful agent for change: Find a champion, convince senior management, enforce expectations, and anticipate and overcome resistance. Companies that depend on Newtonian models for change look for a powerful force for change internally or they reach outside themselves to find consultants who are seen to "carry more weight" because they are external to the current structures. All of these efforts search for and depend on a single change agent or a compact group of change agents to define and execute change, as if the organization were a solid object to be moved from point A to point B.

Online and Offline Systems

The balance between providing service through online ordering and in-store services show the dynamics of change from anywhere in the system. As the number of customers with access to the Internet increases, the number of Internet providers will increase. As the number of providers reaches a critical point, they dilute the customer base. Fewer customers means less profit for providers, so the provider population decreases again. Classical economics assumes this system will result in an equilibrium—a balance—between the numbers of providers and customers. The two numbers would stay constant at this equilibrium number until some other factor influenced the system. Using nonlinear computer models, economists have realized that even this system will not reach a stable equilibrium point. The populations will vary continuously as growth in one population leads to a growth or decline in the other. A change on one side of the boundary results in a change on the other side—a transforming exchange.

> The changes occur in the provider and customer populations, but there is no single controlling factor either internal or external to the system. The interdependencies of the individual providers and customers "control" the behavior of the system as a whole. The same is true of transforming exchanges in organizational settings: Each part of the system responds to changes in other parts, but no single factor determines the behavior of the system as a whole.

In a complex, highly dependent system such as an organization, a solution based on the expectation of a single-point cause of change is doomed to failure. Any individual change agent, regardless of its power or place in the system, is only *one* source of transforming exchanges among a myriad of competing feedback loops. Every part of the system—individual, team, department, corporation, or industry—responds to messages across an infinite number of boundaries. Many of the messages received encourage stability and resistance to changes initiated by a single change agent pushes it. No one participant in the system can override the multiple messages that emerge from the accumulation of all of the other agents in the system.

> A change agent can help a group assess and improve current feedback loops and patterns of behavior by using Method: Feedback Analysis, p. 40.

We saw evidence of this pattern of behavior while working with the research and development (R&D) group for an international manufacturing company. Historically, the company supported two R&D teams. One worked primarily on military and government contracts. Its internal structures and communication mechanisms were fashioned on those of the military—strong and authoritarian leaders, clear roles and lines of accountability, and focus on technological advancements. The other R&D group was associated with the consumer products division. This group had organized to meet the needs of its customers—self-managed teams, close association with marketing and customer service sectors, and focus on usability for products and services.

These two teams were placed together after a massive reorganization. Their needs and cultures were so divergent that, even after two years, the groups continued to function independently. Multiple efforts to force integration were unsuccessful. No one point of power was sufficient to establish a common frame for performance between the two.

When we were invited in to work with the group, we recognized quickly that the impetus for change would have to arise from many different points in the system. Each active agent in this complex system would have to implement his or her own agenda for change. To support this process, we shared the language of complex adaptive systems. Many of the scientists had worked with nonlinear systems in their research, so the science behind the metaphors came easily to them. Our contribution was to convince them that the dynamics they understood in natural systems also shaped the behavior of their organization.

In the course of our work together, the scientists and their managers realized that:

- They did not need a single, coherent picture of the department before they could work together productively;

- They did not need a single source of power or vision to rebuild their teams;

- Differences in management approach and styles of customer interactions were a benefit, not a barrier, to excellent service;

- Individuals could work independently and in groups to build new, more effective structures; and

- The organization of the whole could emerge from the effective work of the individuals and parts of the department.

Individuals and teams across both parts of the organization were able to use the language of CAS to reflect on the multiple forces that shaped their organizational behavior. Each person was encouraged to use the complex interactions to explore new ways to perform, communicate about, and administer daily work. Within a matter of months, the group had not only defined a working organizational structure, but they were well on their way to implementing their new designs.

Leadership and Influence in a CAS

Unlike traditional models of organizational systems, there are no clear system-wide inputs, transformation processes, nor outputs in a CAS. For example, in a healthy CAS, the relationship of a vendor to the customer has mutual interaction and influence. The vendor empathizes with the customers enough to understand their concerns, while the customers recognize the limitations of the vendor's products and services. With an appropriate level of honesty on both sides, the relationship between the vendor and customer moves to new levels of understanding and trust.

A leader can determine her or his role in influencing the three conditions of self-organization by using Method: Leader as Change Agent, p. 45.

In a CAS each agent has autonomy and power over its own actions. Every self-organized group works within its own container, with its own unique differences and idiosyncratic transforming exchanges. In the dynamic relationships, the agents exercise influence to build complex systems. As an agent in the system, the leader participates in her or his own relationships. The environment determines how a leader might use resources of power and influence in these relationships to influence the self-organizing process. For example, if information is scarce, leaders who have information are useful for directing behavior, but when information is plentiful, a flattened organization with peer relationships is more responsive to change.

The current explosion of the Internet marketplace is changing the role of the leader. The new patterns support flat, virtual organizations. They can eliminate the foundation of entire companies and industries in a matter of weeks. To survive in such an environment, organization leaders must elicit the best abilities and insights individuals have to offer. When individual contributors have access to up-to-date information about work flows, production, and quality, they can take over many traditional managerial roles.

Despite the need for maximum worker autonomy to respond to a dynamic environment, a central theme for traditional managers remains: maintain control. Leaders express this wish for control in these ways:

- Requiring sign-off approvals before subordinates can release information;
- Depending on centralized management;
- Using words such as "empowerment" to impose purpose and initiative on workers;
- Ignoring the voices of employees and customers; and
- Developing loyal subordinates and allies to help maintain positions of power and control.

For leaders who like the security of a command-and-control environment, shifting to managing with complexity principles is very difficult. As everyday crises arise, spending time nurturing connections seems like a waste of time. Letting go of control is most difficult. Petzinger (1999) quotes Herb Kelleher, founder and chairman of Southwest Airlines: "If you create an environment where people truly participate, you don't need control. They know what needs to be done and they do it." Petzinger also quotes a Marine Corps publication titled *Command and Control* that calls leadership a process of continuous adaptation:

> "Like a living organism, a military organization is never in a state of stable equilibrium but is instead in a continuous state of flux—continually adjusting to its surroundings . . . . Command and control is not so much a matter of one part of the organization 'getting control over' another as something that connects all the elements together in a cooperative effort. All parts of the organization contribute action and feedback—'command' and 'control'—in overall cooperation. Command and control is thus fundamentally an activity of reciprocal influence—give and take among all parts, from top to bottom and side to side." (p. 182)

> **COMMAND AND CONTROL is thus fundamentally an activity of reciprocal influence—give and take among all parts, from top to bottom and side to side.**

Role of Formal Leader

In a CAS, formal leaders have three jobs: (1) set the containers, (2) focus on significant differences, and (3) foster transforming exchanges. This implies a high degree of mutual influence among all agents, including the formal leaders.

Set Containers

By "setting a container" we mean influencing the environment that shapes the behavior of a system. The container is an attribute of the system that separates it from its environment. Traditional containers include such things as clear goals and expectations, project schedules, budgets, work teams, physical space, or other system boundaries. If a leader maintains the existing culture and power arrangements as manifested in the traditional containers, significant changes will not occur. In a CAS there is always "permanent white water" (Vaill, 1989), where even the process of change is itself changing. New containers related to new clients, new sources of funding, or new diversity in the organization must be recognized and set. Leaders set containers in at least six ways:

1. *Set few specifications.* Leaders must see planning as a process of discovery, filled with ambiguity and possibilities. Rather than instructing the agents on what to do, the leader must allow the team to see what requires attention by identifying a few essential specifications. Leaders must set general requirements for the outcome, but decisions about how to proceed are left to the agents.

   - *Leader's question:* "What minimum specifications will lead to productive outcomes?"

2. *Distribute control.* A CAS has distributed control in a pattern of respectful and trusting relationships. This reduces dependence on any one leader. Openness about issues of control and decision making helps agents agree to undertake responsibilities.

   - *Leader's questions*: "How can I help?" "What do you need?"

3. *Generate a sense of urgency.* Some organizations have developed structures that speed up innovation. Peters and Waterman (1982) called them "skunkworks" because they are generally isolated from the main business to reduce the burdens of maintaining regular business practices. Skunkworks build small containers of time, space, membership, and project focus. Small containers mean fast self-organization.

   SMALL CONTAINERS mean fast self-organization.

   - *Leader's question:* "What do we need to do to meet that deadline?"

4. *Stretch boundaries.* Leaders enlarge boundaries to increase creative options by performing small experiments that encourage learning. Adding new staff and assigning new roles and responsibilities also tend to stretch system boundaries.

   - *Leader's question:* "What's missing?"

5. *Shrink boundaries.* The leader constrains communication when an organization is undergoing change at a rate that cannot be accommodated. Structures, like teams, reduce individual variation, build coherence, and provide frameworks for evaluation. For example, teams channel communications and reduce the number of individual contacts with the environment. By making contracts and agreements on a departmental level, time and costs associated with individual agent activity may be reduced.

   - *Leader's question:* "What can we ignore?"

6. *Decide what business we are in.* Leader discretion determines which markets to pursue, what products and services to provide, and even what physical location is most desirable.

- *Leader's questions:* "Why are we here as an organization?" "What makes us unique?"

All of these strategies allow a leader to shape the speed and patterns of self-organization by managing the container.

Focus on Significant Differences

A second role of the leaders is to focus the resources of the group on the most important differences that will form the emerging patterns. The most important differences are the ones that will shape the most productive patterns. There are at least five ways leaders can focus on these differences.

1. *Explore contradictions.* Leaders should encourage different viewpoints. When tensions emerge, a group should be encouraged to acknowledge and resolve them. When a group maintains tension between polarities of opinions and beliefs, it generates transformations in group members that no one could predict (Olson, 1992).

- *Leader's question:* "How else might we think about this?"

2. *Accept contention and adversity.* In a CAS, a leader should be concerned if there is not conflict. Conflict signals growth and learning, while its absence is a symptom of stagnation and decline.

- *Leader's question:* "What are you holding back?"

3. *Raise tough questions.* Leaders inspire higher levels of performance by inspiring others with vision. They can tell their stories about why the organization is important to them. When a leader reinforces the importance of schedule or budget, agents find new ways to cut costs or reduce unnecessary steps. Frequent requests for reports can also stir action. These are also behaviors used in a mechanistic system, but in a CAS the purpose is to increase connections and action, not to meet a predetermined goal or rigid objective.

- *Leader's question:* "What do you really think?"

4. *Encourage workforce diversity.* Members of a CAS bring a rich tapestry of experience, insights, backgrounds, and cultures. Such differences are essential to maintaining a lively mix of agent activity.

   • *Leader's question:* "Who else needs to be at the table?"

5. *Understand significant differences in the external environment.* Leaders scan the environment for innovations and other differences that can create new patterns. They choose to follow innovations discovered elsewhere or to avoid paths that others have found go nowhere. The leader can also direct the organization's funding of worthy charitable causes and lobby for legislation that furthers the organization's mission.

   • *Leader's question:* "What are the innovations that will create a new pattern for the organization?"

By pursuing these strategies, the leader can conserve a group's energy by focusing on important differences.

Design Transforming Exchanges

Leaders foster co-evolution of all parts of the system when they develop linkages between agents. We call these links transforming exchanges. The leader can influence the design of transforming exchanges in at least four ways.

1. *Encourage feedback.* Beginning with the leaders, everyone in the CAS needs continual feedback about their performance.

   • *Leader's questions:* "How am I doing?" "How are we doing?"

2. *Link communities of practice.* Leaders need to identify and encourage linkage of the communities of practice within the organization as well as linkages with external customers and other stakeholders. Training opportunities and other human development opportunities provide valuable mechanisms for transforming exchanges.

   • *Leader's question:* "What professional networks do you use?"

3. *Reconfigure (loosen or tighten) networks.* Cooperation has to be encouraged among the system agents in cross-functional teams, moving people to new locations, or changing reporting relationships. The leader should maintain balance between having networks that become so tight they are exclusion-

ary and having those that fail to connect agents and thus miss the benefits of a network.

- *Leader's question:* "Is information flow optimal?"

4. *Encourage learning.* The leader must encourage information flow and show interest in the personal and professional development of members of the organization. Learning sources are widely available, such as conferences, innovation fairs, and public classes.

   - *Leader's questions:* "What are your questions?" "Where might you look for answers?"

Supporting exchanges among agents and colleagues (inside and outside of the organization), customers, and other stakeholders is an essential role for management.

Leaders set the conditions for self-organization by watching the formation of containers for the agent interaction, identifying and supporting the significant differences for the emerging patterns in the organization, and supporting the mechanisms that make transforming exchanges possible.

The leader has many options for analyzing and designing effective transforming exchanges. Method: Feedback Analysis on page 40 provides an approach to help assess and improve the loops that allow for transforming exchange.

Change Agent Role

The roiling mass of interconnections described in this chapter can be frustrating but they facilitate the work of the organization change consultant.

Stretching and Folding

A metaphor for the role of a change agent in a CAS is the process of making bread by hand. After the bread dough is mixed, the baker stretches the dough on a table and folds it back on itself. A little flour is added if the dough is sticky, and the whole process is repeated many times. We call this "kneading the dough." The kneading process breaks up and makes uniform the carbon dioxide bubbles from the yeast. The baker puts the dough aside to let it rise and then punches, kneads, pats the dough again, places it in bread pans, lets it rise some more, and finally puts the pans into the oven.

The baker's actions of stretching, folding, and waiting for the rising is a metaphor for the influence a change agent has in a CAS. Just as the baker stretches the dough in many directions, the change agent facilitates the movement of the system agents in many directions at the same time. Just as the baker folds the dough back on itself, the change agent enfolds new information and learning back on itself through transforming exchanges.

Waiting for the dough to rise is a metaphor for the patience required by change agents to allow systems agents to create new pathways, learn from their interactions (stretching), and enfold the learning back into the organization. For example, in one case, in planning a retreat for organizational restructuring, the planning group did all of the work while the change agent was able to sit patiently and respond to an occasional question—a much different role than the active role often taken by consultants to take over and facilitate the process of planning.

As agents interact, what arises cannot be predicted. Our experience is that the outcomes of unfettered interactions have a greater sustainability over a longer time than controlled or forced interactions that may produce desired but ultimately short-lived results.

What are the implications for the role of a change agent? They are summarized in Table 2.1 for the major phases of a change initiative. *Contracting* includes marketing, identifying the client, entering the client system, and contracting for the scope and duration of the work. *Assessing* includes information gathering, feedback, and determining first steps. *Intervening* includes consultant action at the individual, group, or system level. *Evaluating* includes collecting data on outcomes and analyzing and presenting results of the intervention.

Table 2.1. Role of the Change Agent

Change Through Connections			
Phase	**Focus**	**Action**	**Outcome**
Contracting	Agents at all levels	Contract with multiple agents. Learn about leader style, motives, and readiness for change.	First-hand experience of the entangled system; confidence in leader support of change effort.

Table 2.1. Role of the Change Agent, Cont'd

Phase	Focus	Action	Outcome
Assessing	Degree of mutual causality; emerging leadership patterns	Observe interactions. Identify communication and transformation patterns.	Patterns of connections among parts of the system; distribution of leadership in system.
Intervening	Connection of leaders to all agents	Help leaders give up expectations of control. Expand or constrain connections as appropriate.	Adaptation of leaders and agents to new pattern.
Evaluating	Self-organizing patterns; emerging patterns of connection and leadership	Track change over time. Evaluate actions to improve feedback. Use Reflection Evaluation Method (see Chapter 8).	Smoother and more productive interactions; make leadership patterns evident to the system.

Summary

The dynamic interaction and mutual influence of the agents in a CAS was described in this chapter. In such a system, organizational position and title carry a different kind of weight. Influencing people through compensation and financial incentives or perks may create movement, as Herzberg, Mausner, and Snyderman argued in 1959, but not effective motivation for change. In fact, members of a system often view change efforts based on official position with suspicion.

We used to think of change leadership in military metaphors—leading the charge, making an end run around resistance, holding ground, making a run for it, bringing in the big guns. In these metaphors the organization and its inhabitants are seen as inanimate objects that have to be forced into new roles and relationships.

The organic image of the CAS elicits different metaphors for change. Even in the military, leaders are as much affected by the organization as they affect it. Permanent systemic change is impossible until a leader engages personally in the process of change. True leadership toward change depends on individual and immediate connections, personal modeling, and authentic reinforcement.

The interaction of the system agents benefits from leadership behavior to enhance connectivity. Many leaders in organizations know that connectivity comes at a cost, so they shy away from making large investments in learning, communication, and iterative processes. To be successful, the change agent must make the case for the value of adaptability through connectivity.

As we saw in the hospital merger story, a dilemma for consultants in developing a contract is whether system leaders or members desire new pathways and feedback loops for transforming exchange. Opening up areas of investigation in leadership styles, working relationships, appraisal methods, and so on inevitably opens information channels, which some leaders or members have worked hard to keep closed.

In a CAS the primary client who has defined the scope of the initiative (and is usually paying for it) also has the power to stop the change process or turn the emerging CAS into a machine-model organization. The consultant must engage the primary client about his or her motives and readiness for change. The client must be involved in identifying the information channels that are likely to be opened and the transforming exchanges that will be created. The client must be responsible for continuing the process of change. If not, then a fear reaction could set in, and the process will close down before new patterns can emerge.

▶ METHOD: FEEDBACK ANALYSIS

Purpose

During adaptation system agents engage with the environment and with each other to set the stage for transforming exchanges. This method provides a framework for an individual or a group to assess and improve current feedback loops and patterns of behavior.

Preparation

Before completing this activity, a group should understand the role of feedback loops and transforming exchanges in the emergence of systemic behavior. The group must understand the basic characteristics of feedback in a CAS, including the following:

- *Loops* connect across differences (boundaries) in a system;
- Each loop has a *medium* that carries the message (examples include e-mail, phone, meetings, newsletters, and so on);
- The *length* of the feedback loop represents the amount of time that passes between sending a message and receiving a reply;

- The *width* of the loop is determined by the amount of information that can flow through the loop at the same time (for example, a luncheon meeting provides many different kinds of messages, while an e-mail is of more limited width); and

- The *dynamic* of the loop indicates whether it amplifies (encourages) or dampens (discourages) current behavior.

All of these characteristics determine whether a particular feedback loop will be effective or not. Each can be changed to alter patterns of transforming exchanges that build the self-organization of the system.

Distribute several Feedback Analysis Forms (Exhibit 2.1) to each member of the group.

Process

During the activity, the group selects a particular relationship to analyze. Focusing on that single relationship, group members define the feedback loops that currently exist. They describe the medium, length, width, dynamic, and effectiveness of each of the current feedback loops. After describing the current loops, the group considers an alternative loop that might provide more opportunity for transforming exchanges between them and the other participant(s) in the process. The alternative loop is described under the column titled "Proposed Loop."

Debriefing

In discussing the method with a group, the change facilitator should look for:

- *Careful and honest evaluation of existing feedback loops.* How is information shared (medium)? How long does the communication cycle take (length)? How many different kinds of information are transferred (width)? Does the feedback amplify or damp past actions (dynamic)? In what ways is the feedback loop effective and ineffective?

- *Interdependencies among feedback loops.* Feedback loops do not function independently. Face-to-face meetings, memos, e-mails, and voice mail work together to meet the needs of the system agents. During the debriefing, identify which of the current loops depend on each other for their effectiveness.

Exhibit 2.1. Feedback Analysis Form

	Current Loop 1	Current Loop 2	Current Loop 3	Proposed Loop
Medium				
Length				
Width				
Dynamic				
Effective?				
Ineffective?				

- *Focus on significant differences.* Not all feedback is worth the effort. Some feedback loops waste time and energy on issues that are not significant to the work of a group. Part of the analysis of the effectiveness of the feedback loops should include a question about how integral the communication is to specific group outcomes. If the feedback does not focus on significant differences, then perhaps it should be discontinued, not replaced with another loop.

- *Containers within which self-organization may happen.* Feedback is wasted if it does not move toward system transformation. Resources committed to small, closed containers may produce no useful outcome. Resources committed to very large containers may be lost in the complex combination of other voices. Effective feedback loops work within and across container bounds that are most likely to be transformed.

Example

We used this method to great advantage when working with a technical supervisor at an international brokerage firm. His staff complained about his communication skills, but he failed to see the problem. By his report, he spent all of his time communicating with his team. "What," he asked, "would it take to satisfy them?"

The supervisor completed a Feedback Analysis Form and realized that most of his communications were tightly controlled. A copy of his analysis appears in Exhibit 2.2.

His feedback loops with the team were regular and frequent, but they were almost exclusively one-way communications that were opportunities for damping feedback. The more energy he put into such communications, the more frustrated his team members became. Given this analysis, he designed a feedback approach—visiting team meetings—that would allow for positive and two-way communications. The team responded positively to his new mode of communication because they, too, were included in the process. Their interactions became transforming exchanges for everyone. ◀

Exhibit 2.2. Sample Completed Feedback Analysis Form

	Current Loop 1	Current Loop 2	Current Loop 3	Proposed Loop
Medium	Staff meeting	Memos	Status Reports	Visit team meetings
Length	Weekly	Intermittent	Monthly	Weekly
Width	Face-to-face, some chit chat	Formal and narrow	Just the facts	Face-to-face
Dynamic	Damping, one-way	Damping, one-way	Amplifying, one-way	Mixed, two-way
Effective?	Share questions Build team feeling Identify future issues	Gets information out Establishes procedures	Tracks performance Identifies overlap Sets resource needs	TBD
Ineffective?	Repetitive Not well attended Not informative for supervisor	No clear response Throw them away	Throw them away Redundant Ignore overarching issue	TBD

► METHOD: LEADER AS CHANGE AGENT

Purpose

Leaders do have an important role in a complex adaptive system. This method helps a leader determine his or her appropriate role in response to the current situation.

Preparation

To assess the kinds of behavior that would be most appropriate for the leader, the assessment chart in Exhibit 2.3 is useful. The three conditions for fostering a self-organizing system are in Column 1: Containers, Transforming Exchanges, and Significant Differences. In Column 2 the user identifies the current situation. In Column 3 the user identifies the possible changes in the situation. In Column 4 the user lists the various actions a leader might take.

Exhibit 2.3. Leader As Change Agent

Conditions for Self-Organization	Situation:		
	Current	Possible Changes	Leader Action
Containers			
Transforming Exchanges			
Significant Differences			

Process

Exhibit 2.3 is not a prescriptive guide for the leader or other system agents, but rather a display of the activity in a CAS. The patterns that emerge will be influenced by the activities in this matrix. The final outcome cannot be determined because the actions of other stakeholders in the environment are not identified, but it does suggest options for the leader who wants to influence the system.

Example

In retrospect, the matrix would have been useful for the consultants in the hospital merger case at the beginning of this chapter. Exhibit 2.4 identifies what was happening in the case. ◄

Exhibit 2.4. Sample Leader As Change Agent

Conditions for Self-Organization	Situation: Merger of Two Hospitals		
	Current	Possible Changes	Leader Action
Containers	Two organizations; shared geography; different history & culture	One organization; shared history	Sponsor organization-wide experiences to build positive shared history.
Transforming Exchanges	Contract discussions	Many exchanges at multiple places through integration meetings.	Establish cross-organization teams to investigate processes.
Significant Differences	Organization specialization; different values	New services for clients; increase competitiveness	Focus on differences between new company and competition rather than differences within.

When leaders find effective ways to impact the self-organizing process, the process of organization change will move forward. However, these changes are not predictable, so the change agent needs to help clients do their work under the conditions of uncertainty we describe in Chapter 3.

3

Adapt to Uncertainty (Not Predictable Stages of Development)

SELF-ORGANIZATION DOES NOT OCCUR in predictable stages. The interaction of the system agents creates unpredictable patterns that change over time. In turn, these patterns affect how the agents interact with one another in the future. This process moves the system forward into an uncertain future. The evolving path of a project demonstrates this indeterminacy and evolution. Unexpected changes shift the project manager's plan, and the new plan reshapes project activities, which cause future changes to the plan.

In the model of self-organization shown in Figure 3.1, the two arrows have enclosed question marks. One question mark appears before a new pattern is formed to indicate the uncertainty of the evolution of patterns. The second question mark, which appears after the pattern forms, represents the uncertainty of the next and all future interactions of the system agents. This iterative process is nonlinear and emergent. The cycle repeats continually, and each iteration introduces new levels of uncertainty. Because of these nonlinear and surprising cycles, change agents must be willing and able to work in uncertainty.

Figure 3.1. Uncertainty in a CAS

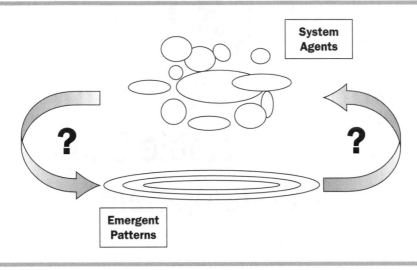

The endless possibilities of the future are dependent on the specific decisions others make, the actions they take, and their interpretations about what they see. Some of the future structures are already known. The Internet, fiberoptics, the space station, global companies, and new organization forms are some examples of currently emerging patterns that will shape the future. How we respond to these new possibilities and to each other will create the patterns of the future.

Although we can build a sketchy view of the future, our expectations provide a distorted view. An example may be helpful here. People who fish with a fish locator see a cone of water. Within the cone, fish are identified as blips on a radar screen. The deeper the water, the larger the space represented by the cone. When blips appear on the screen, the person fishing has no idea where the fish are relative to the boat. The locator simply indicates that there are fish in the vicinity, but it does not tell whether the fish will be caught. Our visions of the future work the same way. We may know that some surprise lies somewhere in the future, but we cannot know exactly what will happen or when it will happen.

The change agent's role in balancing predictability and surprise in self-organizing systems and in helping clients make decisions under conditions of uncertainty is the topic of this chapter.

Nonlinear Organization Change

If organization change were linear, it would proceed in a straight line. Things would get "straightened out" in a series of steps or milestones, as depicted on many project managers' charts. There is a similar linear progression in an automobile with an automatic transmission. It provides the experience of smooth linear motion. There is a predictable relationship between the amount of gas fed to the carburetor and the speed of travel. If these connections are not linear, the wheels spin in mud or on ice, and the experience is unpredictable.

The future of an organization is not a linear projection of the past. The self-organizing nature of human interactions leads to all kinds of surprising, iterative interactions. Small, incremental changes in strategy can produce dramatic changes in outcomes, which can be either positive or negative.

SMALL, INCREMENTAL CHANGES in strategy can produce dramatic changes in outcomes, which can be either positive or negative.

Nonlinear interactions can be positive when a scientist experiments with new product materials. The creative experimenting with 3M's non-sticking glue is a good example. This small innovation made Post-it® Notes possible and earned a huge new market and additional profits for 3M.

Nonlinear interactions can also be negative. Stock market crashes are perfect examples of destructive nonlinear phenomena. A stock begins to drop, stockholders sell to avoid further losses, other stocks drop, more people sell, more loss, more selling. This iterative process will continue, each cycle feeding on the results of the previous one, until some external control mechanism kicks in to disrupt the cycle.

Whether for good or ill, nonlinear patterns of behavior can exaggerate small occurrences into large patterns. But observers cannot usually anticipate what will be amplified or damped in the process or how quickly the change will accumulate. Uncertainty in system behavior emerges when nonlinear interactions exaggerate apparently irrelevant differences to generate wildly unpredictable futures.

One behavioral example of nonlinearity in personal experience arises during multi-tasking. Complex interactions between the tasks lead to learning. Insights from one task feed into the other, which feeds new insights back again. The flashes of insight that emerge and cross boundaries from one task to another indicate nonlinear interaction, and they are certainly not predictable.

Team development demonstrates the same pattern. Nonlinear interactions among group members over time lead to surprising results. The only way to constrain the uncertainty is to constrain interactions and to structure time and tasks.

In such conditions, groups may develop in predictable ways because they, in effect, become like machines.

In these and many other organizational situations, the nonlinear patterns of self-organization generate unpredictable futures. In the midst of the uncertainty, decisions have to be made. A common and logical response is for the complex adaptive system and its leaders to try to reduce uncertainty by excessive planning and control. Although apparently logical, this strategy leads to other complications. System agents feel constrained and underutilized. Leaders must deal with conflicts and new information explicitly and consciously. Valuable resources are consumed in the ongoing control of the system. In many instances, these problems are a high price to pay for an illusion of predictability. To be effective, change agents must develop a degree of comfort with organizational uncertainty. It is a necessary skill and is essential for those who want to influence a CAS. The following story illustrates how efforts to reduce uncertainty can lead to organizational disaster.

▶ STORY: UNPREDICABILITY VS. NEED FOR CONTROL

Jules was the CEO of a large manufacturing and distribution company. In this role, he managed the expectations of a large and diverse board of directors.

Jules had been successful because he held a fundamental belief about his work: Reliability, accountability, and predictability are the hallmarks of a good manufacturing operation. These beliefs moved Jules up the management chain and into his position of authority.

He used the same principles with the board. Every meeting had a full agenda. The group moved through the agenda with clear expectations. Votes were always unanimous because Jules did his homework to ensure that proposals were acceptable to everyone before he put them on the table. All in all, he ran an orderly ship.

In spite of good performance and a smooth history, some board members felt powerless and manipulated when major decisions were laid before them. Initially the concerns were expressed informally and in private. Over time, however, the dissatisfaction grew. The board chair called for a meeting that would be structured as a dialogue. No one would be expected to make final decisions, but everyone would have an opportunity to speak and to be heard.

Jules was adamant that such a meeting not take place. He could not imagine beginning a three-hour meeting without knowing what would be discussed, what would be said, and what decisions would be made. He delayed scheduling the meeting, saying that other concerns were pressing for immediate attention.

The board's dissatisfaction increased, and Jules' ability to control the behavior of the board diminished over time. Ultimately he was replaced, and the board retained a more collaborative, flexible CEO.

Jules was so uncomfortable with uncertainty that he could not let go of the reins of self-organization. As long as the board was willing to work within his constraints, Jules' strategy was successful. The diverse perspectives on the board, however, were not willing to work within such narrow and pre-defined bounds. They wanted to have transforming exchanges so that they could examine for themselves the real situation and the differences that were shaping the performance of the company.

Jules' need for control closed his eyes to the energy and wisdom of the system as a whole. ◄

Lesson of the Story

Some uncertainties have to be embraced if an organization is to adapt to changing environments. Managers like Jules are correct in believing that some organizational activities and dynamics have to be predictable. When a situation involves a small or closed system container, when transforming exchanges are tightly controlled, and when significant differences are few, the future path of a system is relatively predictable. For example, the standard operating procedures on a manufacturing assembly line should hold few surprises. Jules' mistake was that he tried to sustain the same degree of certainty in his relationship with the board.

Expectations of predictability cannot be met when a system is open to self-organization. Predictability decreases markedly when widening a container (broader mission to serve new clientele), establishing transforming exchanges (cross-department committees), or integrating new significant differences (new professional specialists). In such circumstances, the future becomes indeterminate.

Consulting to Uncertainty

Change agents add value when they help organizations and leaders like Jules respond appropriately to the uncertainty in a system. Three strategies can help the change agent support effective action in an indeterminate future:

- Identify areas for self-organization;
- Identify areas for rational approaches; and
- Share uncertainty with clients.

The Method: Decision Making Under Conditions of Uncertainty, p. 63, helps the change agent and client to sort through many organizational issues to determine the appropriate approach to making decisions.

Identify Areas for Self-Organization

New information or new ways of thinking about familiar information provide a picture of unpredictable patterns. By helping the organization recognize its own unpredictability, the change agent moves it to a place far from certainty and closer to creativity, where it becomes highly sensitive to small changes. Knowing which aspects of the organization are already self-organizing and which have the potential for self-organization helps the clients to amplify tiny fluctuations or disturbances throughout the system. Organizational aspects that are allowed to self-organize have outcomes that are inherently unpredictable, but that are adaptive to the changing environment (Stacey, 1992).

Identify Areas for Rational Approaches

Change agents often feel the need to promise predictability to the client and strive to achieve this by using rational methods for inherently unpredictable situations. If the organization uses cause-and-effect analysis, it decreases the awareness of uncertainty, collapses the problem/decision space, and limits the possibility that creative solutions will emerge. In a CAS, change agents could help determine whether issues can be addressed with rational, analytical methods, or whether complexity methods are needed. For example, by asking whether the consequences of a decision are predictable, the change agent helps the group let go of using rational methods that can lead to false certainties.

Share Uncertainty with Clients

Any change intervention must be designed to complement the current state of the system. The change agent must resist the urge for certainty long enough to be clear about what kind of approach is appropriate. Here the uncertainty of the client meets the uncertainty of the change agent.

Ideally, change agents share their own uncertainty and feelings with clients as they listen to the clients' concerns and feelings. This builds the level of trust and creates a mutually influencing process in deciding about next steps. Schein (1999) calls this "accessing our ignorance."

For example, in a consultation with the research division of a computer manufacturer, our goal was to improve cross-disciplinary teamwork. The first step was interviewing the top managers. The next step was to decide whom to involve from the staff. It was essential to keep the container (number of interviewees) small enough to allow for optimal interaction and emergence within the project budget constraints. As consultants, we could not know what mix was best. By sharing the problem with a division director, we used his knowledge of the system to overcome our unknowns and to format the staff interviews. One group of professionals was very heterogeneous by background and specialization. One-on-one interviews were essential to capture the range of their insights. Another group included members from similar backgrounds, and focus groups sufficed to collect information about their perspectives. The ultimate design was successful because it married our certainty about self-organizing design with the division director's certainty about his current situation. In this way, we overcame part of the uncertainty that was inherent in the system.

No Sequence of Events

Developmental models of groups or organizations are based on images of predictable sequences of events. The expectation for predictable development is embedded in cultural myths, religious practice, educational theory, and economic development. The models assume that the issues of one stage will be resolved and that the group or organization will move to the next stage. Ultimately, the system will reach a level of high performance after moving through a series of structured developmental stages.

A complex adaptive system does not admit to any certainty of steps in a process or predictable, staged outcomes. To expect a predictable developmental path is to deny the reality of complex adaptation. Agents interact according to free will and self-interest. External forces affect the system. New and different options appear to reshape the landscape. Each moment of evolution represents multiple possible paths toward an adaptive future.

The self-organizing view does not deny the usefulness of staged models of development, but it limits their applicability. Development of an individual or group over a short period of time may fall into a discernible developmental pattern. Assumptions of a predictable developmental process on a small scale can be quite helpful. When a system becomes complex enough, however, the underlying stability disappears, and the step-wise process breaks down. What is left is unpredictable adaptation.

When an organization reaches the point of unpredictability, typically leaders and employees alike fear negative outcomes and unintended consequences. In systems that value accountability, leaders and members face a quandary: Who is going to be accountable if things go awry? Although these reactions are understandable, the system agents are asking the wrong question.

In an unpredictable CAS, all agents are accountable all of the time for the information they share or withhold and for their actions, but they are not accountable for the outcomes. Their challenge and opportunity is to be explicit about their intentions and continually to test the results of their behavior, but not to be paralyzed or guilty about unfavorable outcomes over which they had no control to begin with.

The agents in many organizations are programmed to follow procedures and routines in order to maintain readiness, but when a rapid response to unusual events is required, the agents adapt without certainty about the outcome. For example, although a fire or rescue team responds to emergencies with a well-thought-out and rehearsed plan, once on the scene they adapt to the specific situation. In football, a quarterback may call out a change in the play a second before the ball is snapped in response to how he sees the defensive team lined up. In the case of broken plays, all of the players' moves are adaptive.

Speed of Adaptation

The outcome of a self-organizing process is determined by the complex interactions within the system and is usually unknown to the change agent. It is possible, however, for a change agent to influence the speed of change.

The rate of change in a self-organizing system is affected by the size of the container, the frequency of the transforming exchanges, and the number of significant differences. A change agent can adjust these conditions to shift the speed of the self-organizing process.

Container Management

Creating a larger container slows down the change process because the energy required for new organization is dispersed. Shrinking the container speeds up the change process because the potential and focus for change are concentrated. For example, to speed up a group's issue-resolution process, a consultant can shrink the size of the container by setting up a "fishbowl" in the center of the room. The intensity and pace of the discussion is increased as group members with the most interest in the issue join the fishbowl. The issue becomes more sharply defined, and the competing alternatives become clearer. To facilitate a slower, more deliberate, decision process, the facilitator can enlarge the container by disbanding the fishbowl and engaging the whole group.

Briggs and Peat (1999) describe a similar practice in the "talking circle" of the Blackfoot people. In the organizational center of their community where they make their decisions, they always leave a gap for the new to enter. Briggs and Peat say that this gap represents the creative openness always present within self-organization.

Exchange Management

When control is distributed throughout a system, the individual agents are able to adapt readily to new information. For example, a networked virtual organization has many agents who can respond to changes in their unique environments. In effect, the system has multiplied the number of transforming exchanges to support self-organization. The large numbers of connections provide flexibility and agility to respond to change. Each agent becomes an engine for self-organization because he or she makes transforming exchanges with many others. Change, then, can occur in many different places. If these agents (leaders and members) of an organization are connected by transforming exchanges and leadership does not shut down a self-organizing process, the whole organization will quickly increase its complexity and capacity to adapt.

Petzinger (1999) describes emergence and self-organization as a continuing process of adaptation in a real-time world of global business. Technologies, markets, and relationships emerge and disappear amid a flurry of instant communication. Increasing autonomy and responsibility of employees increases the speed of adaptation. In his interviews with hundreds of business people in industries all over North America, Petzinger observed multiple situations in which productivity soared after employees took over production scheduling and problem solving. In one company, employees who acted on ever-changing customer cues were compared to amoebae that flow with the environment and continually reshape their bodies.

Lewin and Regine (2000) present another example. Monsanto, the chemical company, transformed from a mechanical to an organic mode of operation in ways that follow the principles of complexity science. CEO Bob Shapiro pushed the organization into a state of uncertainty as a way of finding new, more adaptable, creative ways of operating in the new environment. He resisted prioritizing the many challenges, saying to employees: "We have to do them all, and you are going to have to figure out how to do that." Shapiro was astonished by how quickly people were self-organizing, for example, posting proposals for a project they cared about and inviting others to join in (Lewin & Regine, 2000, p. 215).

If the supervisors in a traditional organization try to retain their control over employee behavior, as control begins to be distributed widely, top leadership must help supervisors let go. For example, when we consulted to a client about improving communication and teamwork, we facilitated a one-day retreat using appreciative inquiry methods (Watkins, 2001). The retreat was successful in identifying the need for changes in communication practices. Shortly after the retreat, an employee proposed a temporary task group to develop specific changes in her division. The supervisor shot down the suggestion with little or no discussion. The employee was devastated. Word reached top management, and the management group met to discuss how to support employee initiatives. Within a year the managers improved feedback loops with the employee group and the supervisor adjusted to the new patterns of employee self-initiation.

Managing Significant Differences

The number of focal differences also affects the rate of change. When an organization or group focuses on too many things at the same time, the self-organizing impetus is diluted. Energies move in many directions, and none of them receives sufficient resources to generate new structures. Small numbers of significant differences, however, tend to focus energy for change and accelerate the transformations through self-organization.

A skunkworks team structure is a perfect example of this strategy to speed up change. A small team (few individual differences) comes together for a specific task (few competing objectives) in a single space (no geographical differences) with a tight timeline (no time for distractions). In this constrained environment, the team focuses its energy on a very small number of significant differences and moves rapidly toward new and creative solutions.

Paradoxically, using large-group technology also speeds up the change process. The large-group attendees and design form a new container. When a Future Search or other large-group event (Bunker & Alban, 1996) is held, it compresses the existing containers in the organization in a single room. All departments and work groups are present, or at least represented. For this reason, ideas and agreements that flow from such large-group events have a wide ownership in the organization, and the system-wide change process is accelerated. As a CAS, a large-group event puts the system into a small container and defines the transforming exchanges so that the differences can be articulated. Such an environment accelerates the self-organizing process.

The "Right" Speed for Change

Groups and organizations have choices about their rate of adaptation. They can shrink their containers, support unfettered agent interaction, and focus on a few significant differences to increase the speed of adaptation to the environment. On the other hand, they can choose to maintain a large container, controlled interactions, and multiple significant differences to slow down or even stop adaptation. Either choice has consequences. Either choice has merit. Ultimately, as in most aspects of a CAS, finding a balance between the two that fits with the balance in the environment will ensure the right amount of change and stability.

Three factors should influence the desired speed of change in a CAS. As change agents design the conditions for self-organization, they should consider these three factors: (1) capacity of the system to absorb change, (2) history of the change process in the system, and (3) pace of change in the environment.

Rate of change should be gauged to the capacity of the organization to absorb it. Because this capacity is initially unknown, the change agent must experiment with incremental interventions and adaptations. Although change agents must stretch the limits of the organization's expectations, they must also recognize that change that comes too fast results in no change at all if individuals and groups disconnect from the change process.

The historical experiences of the organization also should help determine the appropriate rate of change. Changes in the *recent* past will affect the energy available in the system to respond to new change initiatives. Changes in the *distant* past will appear as patterns of expectation and interaction in the habitual stories and interactions of the system.

Finally, and most importantly, the rate of change of the environment must influence the preferred rate of change within an organization. In high-tech markets, the system has to change at the same rate as the environment. For example, successful "dot-com" companies change their strategies and tactics at the click of a mouse.

EFFORTS TO MAKE changes must be synchronized with these external forces if the transformation efforts are to be successful.

Clients, suppliers, stockholders, neighborhood cultures, and political power structures are all interrelated through organization dynamics. Efforts to make changes must be synchronized with these external forces if the transformation efforts are to be successful. Too rapid change will threaten relationships on which the organization depends. Too slow change will stifle the possibilities in an uncertain future.

Change Agent Role

To be effective, a change agent must embrace the inevitable uncertainty that comes with working in a CAS. Consultants must contain their own anxiety about uncertainty while helping clients face an uncertain future. Change agents help a system move from certainty to uncertainty and back again. For example, a budget process is open and uncertain as participants compete for resources, but end points are needed in order to develop and implement a budget. A summary of the role of the change agent in helping clients adapt to uncertainty is in Table 3.1.

Table 3.1. Role of the Change Agent

	Adapt to Uncertainty		
Phase	**Focus**	**Action**	**Outcome**
Contracting	Primary client's tolerance for ambiguity	Set realistic expectations about how much certainty and predictability are possible in near-, mid-, and long-term	Client satisfaction that change agent understands the emerging nature of his or her business and organization
Assessing	Identification of predictable and uncertain aspects of system	Analyze the container, transforming exchanges, and differences in systems	Focus on the rate of change and adjust container, exchanges, and difference
Intervening	Shift self-organizing conditions to shape speed of change	Alter conditions; observe and evaluate effects	Shifted change dynamics within the organization
Evaluating	Capacity of the system agents to adapt to changing circumstances	Measure the response time between a shock to the system and development of stable responsive mechanisms	If the response time is minimal, the organization is successfully adapting

Notes on Intervening for Change Agents

Some useful guidelines for change agents to fully participate with the system in times of uncertainty follow:

- Use an iterative redesign approach with constant experimenting on the system as a whole.

- Encourage relatively small organization subunits (containers) in which relationships can develop.

- Encourage acting and responding to actions taken by others. The rule is, "Try something, evaluate its impact, and then try something else." Trying to figure out exactly what will happen leads to "analysis paralysis." Find the courage to act.

- Acknowledge the feelings of system members. Support their discomfort and encourage development of trusting relationships with other agents. Allow a sense of adventure to arise. Denny Gallagher (2000), an experienced OD consultant, sees the challenge as "getting people to be comfortable with their level of discomfort."

- Trust that emergent solutions will occur without pushing ahead with a decision. Help managers find a safe place to explore the personally challenging concepts of emergence.

- Reflect on the significant differences that shaped the current self-organized structure. Use the participants' experiences of historical adaptation to build their models for the future.

- With the client, experience what it is like to self-organize into a more productive group.

Notes on Evaluating for Change Agents

It is inherently difficult to evaluate in an unknowable future. Change agents can help themselves and their clients with these guidelines:

- In a system of uncertainty, it does not make sense to establish some future point and measure progress to that point.

- Every CAS at any point in time is unique, so measuring against competitors or colleagues by benchmarking is not useful either.

- History, however, helps us to evaluate the present. The question is fairly simple: "Are we better today than we were yesterday?" Some management theorists reject this approach because it depends on a rear-view mirror. In an uncertain world, however, the only clear view is the one that looks back, so use the historical view, even while recognizing its limitations.

Summary

In this chapter we discussed the development of a CAS as an unpredictable process moving the system into an uncertain future. The alternative patterns of the future emerge in a nonlinear process that is not a projection of the past. Being a change agent in such a system requires letting go of expectations of predictability. By mirroring a system's unpredictability, a change agent moves the system to a place where it is sensitive to small changes. By avoiding giving solutions and sharing their own uncertainties, change agents help the client to identify solutions that are relevant for the system.

Instead of developing in predictable stages, CASs adapt in different ways. By managing the three conditions of self-organization (container, difference, and exchange) a change agent can increase or decrease the speed of change.

▶ METHOD: DECISION MAKING UNDER CONDITIONS OF UNCERTAINTY[2]

Purpose

Different decision-making processes are appropriate in different levels of uncertainty. In Figure 3.2 we present a model that is useful to classify decisions in terms of their levels of uncertainty.

Figure 3.2. Decision Making Under Conditions of Certainty and Uncertainty

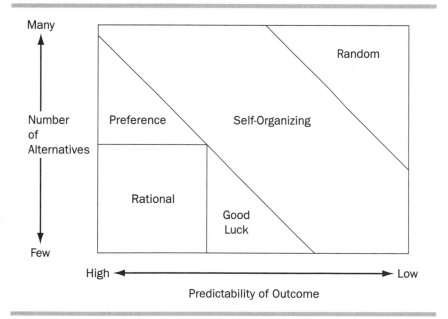

---

[2]This model was inspired by the Stacey Agreement and Certainty Matrix in Zimmerman, Lindberg, and Plsek, 1998, pp. 136–143.

The model in Figure 3.2 can be used to classify decisions to help a team select its approach to decision making. Understanding the two dimensions of the model also aids communication about the decision-making process. The model allows the team to use techniques that are most appropriate, given the complexity and uncertainty of the issues.

Preparation

The dimension of *predictability of outcome* classifies decisions as to their likely outcomes, that is, whether the individuals or group has a high or low degree of certainty about the outcome. Low-certainty decisions may be new to the organization or ones that require an unproven methodology. High-certainty decisions are those that are familiar, repetitive, and cyclical, or ones that depend on thoroughly tested methods.

The second dimension identifies the *number of alternatives* available. Few alternatives narrow the decision toward certainty. If there are only two alternatives, there is at least a fifty/fifty chance of choosing the right one. With few alternatives, it is easier to make comparative cost/benefit calculations. Many alternatives mean greater uncertainty because resources and time are usually insufficient to investigate them all, even if the possibilities were known. The size of each area within the model varies according to the degree of constraint within the organization. A highly constrained organization would have a large area for "rational" decisions. A CAS would have a large area of "self-organizing."

Five Categories of Decisions

Within this model are five separate types of decisions: *rational, preference, good luck, random,* and *self-organizing.*

Rational: High Predictability; Few Alternatives

Rational decisions can be made in systems when there are few alternatives with highly predictable outcomes. Many of the linear methods, such as sales trends, customer satisfaction surveys, productivity measures, or quality indicators, can be used to gather data and to analyze and predict the likely future for issues in this category. This is the area of efficiency and stability. In this category, anxiety is usually low, and the decisions are made comparatively easily and rapidly.

Preference: High Predictability; Many Alternatives

In this category there are many desirable and feasible alternatives, all of which appear to lead to predictable outcomes. The alternatives are a matter of preference or influence. Some alternatives give more advantage to one or another part of the system. Values, beliefs, and other subjective criteria are involved. Making a decision in this domain often requires negotiation, compromise, or exertion of political influence.

Good Luck: Low Predictability; One or Few Alternatives

In this category, decision outcomes are not predictable, but there are few alternatives. If a decision has to be made, it is done with hope or faith that it is correct and will lead to a desired outcome. In football, desperation plays late in the game are referred to as "Hail Mary" passes. The person or group making the decision is under pressure and does not have any other viable alternative, so taking a chance on the only course of action is preferable to inaction.

Random: Low Predictability; Many Alternatives

When there are many different alternatives and low predictability of outcome, the organization is at the state of randomness. There are no complex similarities between behavior patterns in one part of a system and another. For all that is known, any option is equal in value to any other. This state is seen in early creative stages of product development or premature business ventures. The process is somewhat like searching the universe for signs of life by monitoring radio waves. There are many possible paths, but no indication that one would be more fruitful than another. Doing nothing is one alternative, but doing something—anything—may provide information about the relative viability of options. Searching for patterns in the randomness is a better path than inaction.

Self-Organizing: Complexity

In Figure 3.2 the area between randomness and the areas handled by traditional decision-making methods is the area of self-organizing decisions—the area of complexity. The decision approach here inevitably involves a high level of interaction among organizational agents. For example, leaders who wish to improve their decision making or increase the level of trust can initiate feedback sessions from employees. A consultant may gather anonymous data from the staff and engage the leader and staff to find patterns in the data. Without the participation of the staff, the leader would be hard-pressed to determine the specific behavior that affects the level of trust in the organization and effectiveness of the leader. This kind of work involves the kinds of nonlinear methods and practice we describe throughout the book, focusing on containers, differences, and exchanges.

Process

In a group meeting, the members work with pre-existing lists of issues or they generate such a list. The issues are then divided among subgroups of attendees for analysis and classification into the decision-making model. The subgroup results are posted, and attendees vote on the issues of most interest to them by placing up to five dots. This process narrows the list of issues to one or two in each part of the model. The identified issues are then discussed in the large group to determine whether the issue has been appropriately classified. If the group can agree on a classification, members then begin to brainstorm methods or approaches that are appropriate to the kind of action that is required. In the case of general disagreement, the issue is reclassified, restated, or tabled.

Example

The following story describes the model at work.

A group of senior managers in the transportation industry had developed a list of twenty-four issues. They wished to undertake strategic planning but had no consensus about which issues needed priority attention. Their history was to work hard on the simpler issues and postpone discussions on the critical value-laden issues facing the group. During an offsite workshop, the consultant presented the Decision Model. The twenty-four issues, which had been identified earlier as priority issues, were divided among four small groups. The participants were asked to think through their assigned issues and sort them into the five categories of the model: *rational, preference, good luck, random,* and *self-organizing.* The results were tabulated and displayed to the group, which then chose a problem/question in each category for discussion. They were as follows:

- *Rational:* "What are reasonable timelines for the data acquisition?"

- *Preference:* "What data is essential and necessary to evaluate or measure the efforts of the organization?"

- *Good Luck:* "Provide relief to an already stretched field staff operation that believes it is being stretched even further."

- *Random:* "How will the new weather patterns affect our costs?"

- *Self-Organizing:* "Make our customers more responsible for screening and evaluating their drivers."

The group discovered that its discussions were clearer than usual. Group members knew how they should go about making a decision because the methods matched the complexity of the issue. As they worked, several issues moved from one part of the model to another as the number of alternatives increased or as the group became more uncertain about the outcomes of any single alternative.

Other Uses of the Model
We have also used this model:

- To classify issues that were likely to arise during the coming calendar or budget year.

- To see the value of treating a decision as a self-organizing decision (and many are).

- To help groups see that both linear and nonlinear methods may be useful in making decisions.

- To clarify whether the system needs to increase or decrease the level of uncertainty. ◄

The model of decision-making helps clients adapt to uncertainty by using methods of change that are appropriate to the issue and by not attempting to achieve levels of certainty on issues that are not predictable in a CAS. The alternative to trying to control a system to achieve certain outcomes is to let the goals, plans, and structures emerge from the interactions in the system, which we explore in Chapter 4.

4

Emerging Goals, Plans, and Structures (Not Clear, Detailed Plans or Goals)

WHEN AN ORGANIZATION IS VIEWED as a machine, the structural principles are detailed and difficult. Elaborate structures, processes, plans, and clear specifications are required to keep a machine running. The organizing principles of a complex adaptive system are surprisingly simple. As various agents in diverse environments interact, complex patterns emerge across the system that are striking in contrast to mechanistic organization principles.

"Complicated" comes from the Latin word "plic" which means "to fold" (Lissack & Roos, 1999). The process of folding hides facets of the system and crams more detail into a crowded space. With a machine-like view of organizations, overarching goals are lost in detailed plans, structures, and processes.

"Complex" comes from the Latin word "plex" meaning "to weave." Weaving makes use of connections and mutual dependencies. In a CAS, the system agents work with short lists of simple rules to "weave" the current patterns into patterns of the future.

In a *machine-like organization* where everything is *complicated*, the implementation of plans is often thwarted by hidden relationships. Only a few people know the reasoning and steps that lead to decisions and outcomes. Most have to guess about relevance, meaning, and measurement. Most have no idea whether expectations and goals are wise or even attainable.

A *complex adaptive system*, on the other hand, is built from the local behavior of the system agents. The complex *interweaving* that emerges over the history of the organization holds within itself the secrets of success. The building blocks of relationships, information transactions, and connections are known to those who participate in them. Argentine Saunders Craig (2000), an international OD consultant who has worked in many diverse systems, has a favorite saying: "The answer is in the room." The interaction of the agents "in the room" brings out "the answers" and makes them explicit.

ALTHOUGH THE OUTCOME may be difficult to understand in its woven patterns, paradoxically it will be easier for everyone who is involved to understand, re-create, and transform.

In developing a *complex*, rather than a *complicated*, organization, change agents facilitate linkages among system agents, leaders, and outside stakeholders. Although the outcome may be difficult to understand in its woven patterns, paradoxically it will be easier for everyone who is involved to understand, re-create, and transform.

In this chapter we explore how planning, organizing, and control, the major traditional functions of management, are manifested in a CAS. In contrast to traditional systems, arbitrary beginnings, endings, and structures are not imposed. The reality is that plans, structures, controls, and even vision emerge from the interactions of the system agents. The role of the change agent is to reflect on actions and experimentation, not end points.

To help a client understand how a CAS will self-organize, the Method: Self-Organizing Exercise, p. 81, is recommended. The experience reveals organization dilemmas and helps frame new solutions.

Figure 4.1 shows the change agent in the midst of system agent interaction in which the emerging goals, plans, and structures always have some degree of uncertainty.

Figure 4.1. Emerging Goals, Plans, and Structures

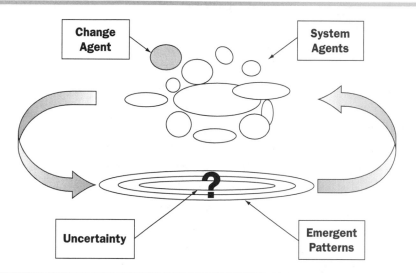

▶ CASE: KNOWLEDGE MANAGEMENT FIRMS

In most professional service and knowledge-based businesses, the most valuable knowledge is held by groups of individuals. These individuals, aggregated into teams, create solutions and collective understandings that are greater than the sum of their parts. These groupings may be formal, informal, or some combination of the two. They include engagement teams, practitioners sharing a geographic location, client service teams that work with the same client organization over time, or industry or functional communities of practitioners devoted to the collaborative development of problem-solving expertise (Manville, 1999).

For example, most of the "Big Six" professional services firms are loosely organized around geographical business units. Staff is highly mobile, belonging to multiple formal and informal networks, such as practices (tax, accounting, consulting), special initiative teams, client service teams, and regional collaborations. Staffing coordinators assemble a variety of teams to work with different clients over a period of time. The teams frequently cross the organization's geographical boundaries to work on projects sponsored by various practices.

Because outcomes of knowledge creation are nonlinear, it is difficult to predict success. There are no guarantees that an aggregation of specific people will produce valuable innovations. From a CAS perspective one can create a context for groupings to form and perpetuate themselves. Such strategies could replace internal hierarchies with internal "markets" that produce knowledge with experiments that will either succeed or fail. Agents with no prescribed future can reorganize and reconfigure themselves without any predetermined plan.

Knowledge management firms are examples of how a CAS lets goals, plans, and structures evolve. The scope (container) of the organization and its teams changes over time. Significant differences today become insignificant tomorrow. Transforming exchanges abound. To develop a traditional strategic plan in such an environment would be a delusion. Instead, these self-organizing systems focus on processes that encourage future realities to unfold. ◀

Planning in a CAS

Some organizational planning is necessary, even when prediction is impossible. When an organization functions as a machine, planning and controlling make most sense. Scheduling, monitoring, organizing, directing, and a range of other hands-on management functions are appropriate to absorb or reduce uncertainty and control processes. When an organization is a complex adaptive system, however, the expectation of being in control is a dangerous illusion.

In a CAS, resources must be devoted to understanding the present. What is happening in the present? What do we do better *right now*? What have been our patterns of success in the past? Planning in a CAS is a set of processes to encourage, facilitate, and evaluate organizational experiments. Rather than predicting strategies, complex adaptive planning generates emergent strategies.

IN ORDER TO ASSURE quality or productivity in meeting the needs of the customer, an organization must define small containers in which things are predictable and closed.

Given this emergent image of planning, changes in strategic direction survive if they work. Failures are quickly discarded. In this interactive process, both the expected and the unexpected emerge. By responding to the unexpected, the strategic direction is created anew every day. Agents try combinations of approaches until they find ones that work. Often these innovations occur at the outer edges of a CAS, where system agents have maximum freedom for experimentation.

In order to assure quality or productivity in meeting the needs of the customer, an organization must define small containers in which things are predictable and closed. These production units, for example, are important subsets of the whole organization. Their outputs can be measured and managed with some traditional management methods. It is important, however, to realize that these components are only a part of the larger CAS. The methods and culture in these units should not be imported to the complex adaptive aspects of the organization.

For example, in bringing together three disciplinary groups to resolve their turf issues, a manager wisely avoided refereeing among the three groups. He convened a group of representatives of all three disciplines, gave them the information about the agency's resources and requirements, and asked them to develop the plan for working together. The carrot was that none of them would receive additional resources until they developed a plan. This formed a tight container to encourage rapid self-organization. It led to several successful collaborative projects that have become a regular part of the division's operations. The three groups that designed the collaborative procedures now encounter substantially fewer turf disputes. Other divisions in the company have modified the collaborative solutions to fit their specific needs.

In another case, we consulted with a new CEO about his mandate to develop a strategic plan. The CEO already knew that in the rapidly changing environment the time and money to develop a plan would be better spent in action on the strategic issues that had already been identified. We helped him develop a presentation to explain his approach to various stakeholder groups, including his board of directors and employees. Everyone agreed that action, rather than extensive planning, was the most productive course.

Vision in a CAS

Visioning enables members of a CAS to know who they are, what they do well, and in what directions they want to move. Developing a vision in a CAS requires understanding the present dynamics and letting system members build possibilities for the future. Vision emerges from the space where order and disorder cross over, in the rich interplay of experiences, thoughts, and connections of system agents.

For example, our work in one organization to develop better communications and teamwork began with a one-day retreat where cross-disciplinary groups developed an appreciative vision, based on what individual members of the group reported as times when they have been challenged and excited by their work. An example of a vision statement follows:

> "We are a multidisciplinary team that recognizes that everyone's contribution is critical. We are committed to each other and to our work, which requires proactive leadership, mutual respect, trust, cooperation, and commitment to our objective. We talk to each other, we listen, and we have *FUN* doing it."

This vision statement grew out of the group's current reality. In subsequent meetings they were able to bridge to the organization envisioned in the statement. The leadership group was able to connect its own personal expression of vision and values to the emerging vision in the organization. In the day-to-day work following the retreat, the interacting interpretations of the vision in transforming exchanges created a basis for day-to-day improved communication and teamwork.

Unfortunately, in most organizations, efforts are made to turn the vision into outcomes and goals. Then the goals and outcomes have to be translated into action. Doing so negates the adaptability and richness of the source of the vision—the interaction of significant differences through transforming exchanges in the system container.

Brenda Zimmerman (Zimmerman, Lindberg, & Plsek, 1998) talks about a "good enough" vision that recognizes the impossibility of a clear and explicit vision of the future in an inherently unpredictable system. The best we can do is "good enough," and then we need to start moving—acting—and watching for patterns and direction to emerge. Following are some examples of this principle in action:

- Beginning a group meeting with just enough explicit norms to get started;
- Receiving a lot of feedback and selecting just two or three things to focus on; and
- Disseminating information, from top leaders for example, today rather than later.

Goal Setting in a CAS

For the purposes of work (projects and interventions), we can construct arbitrary beginnings and endings. We must do so in the full knowledge that these are imposed, intentional, imagined breaks in the flow of pattern formation and individual transformation. For example, if a plan is needed for software development, it is better to take what you know, establish a goal, and then reshape as you go along. Do not wait until you have a perfect plan.

In complex adaptive systems, even if we know the initial conditions in detail, we cannot predict the end state of the system reliably. The appropriate image is one of emergence, in which each moment moves into the next to define new options and possibilities. Every beginning is indeed an ending, and every ending is a beginning. In fact, we can think of each point in time as contributing something vital to the flow of reality.

Structures in a CAS

Just as the interaction of the agents generates an unclear end point and frustrates strategic planning efforts in a CAS, so does the interaction of the agents lead to unpredictable structures and organizing principles. The structures that do emerge are resilient and quite capable of reorganizing in response to both small and large events.

Goldstein (1994) tells the classic story of a school of fish that illustrates this phenomenon. In a school of fish, because control is distributed throughout the system:

- A school of fish does not have a boss.
- The independent agents (fish) have the capacity to learn new and adaptive strategies.
- The school of fish reacts to a stimulus (threat) faster than any individual fish can react.
- The school, as a whole, has capacities and attributes that are not explainable by the capacities and attributes of the individual agents.
- If there were a smart "boss" fish, this centralized control would result in a school reacting more slowly than the fastest fish could respond.

Computer simulations of human systems such as automobile traffic patterns also demonstrate that when control is distributed among a population, the outcomes emerge from a process of self-organization, rather than being designed and controlled externally.

Delegated Authority in a Hierarchy

Some organizations with a history of a bureaucratic, hierarchical structure have delegated authority to imposed team structures (quality circles, TQM, re-engineering). The hierarchy imposed these structures; they were not emergent. For this reason, the structures could be withdrawn or disbanded if top managers were not pleased with results. Such delegated authority is insufficient to meet the organizational needs in rapidly changing and open environments.

For example, a large publishing company introduced TQM with much fanfare and a large number of cross-functional teams. Each team had a mandate to explore areas of concern to employees. When the first team ventured into the area of performance appraisal and compensation (an organizational "sacred cow"), it was quickly shut down. The message spread throughout the organization that management was not serious about team-based decision making, and the energy of the initiative rapidly dissipated.

Emerging Structures

When structures are allowed to emerge in participative processes, they are more adaptive and more resilient in dealing with changes to the environment. For example, in a CAS, some self-organized teams dissolve and new ones are formed. At the same time, the whole organization constrains the freedom of the teams, so they do not take arbitrary actions. Even when such an organization breaks up, employees leave, or the teams are restructured, the parts and the whole continue to exist and emerge. For example, when personnel leave companies with a strong culture, such as Control Data, Digital Equipment Corporation, or the Navy Seals, and join small companies, they carry an imprinting of procedures, lessons, and values with them that the new organizations value. Personal friendships and identities established in the previous culture are never lost.

Spider Plant Metaphor

Self-organized structures are not always simply rational. The central offices of some organizations could be compared to the central stalk of a spider plant (see box that follows). It nurtures and supports the clusters at the ends of its many tentacles.

Computer technology enables countless transforming exchanges between the central office and the various departments, branches, and parts.

When customers contact any part of the organization, they can be connected automatically to the central office or to any selected department. As the parts of the system provide feedback to the central office, they identify new significant differences that enhance the opportunity for self-organization in all parts of the system.

Morgan (1997) predicted the demand for "remote" management in which units grow to only a certain size. Further growth occurs when new groups are established. These interdependent units are held together by a shared set of simple rules. The rules form a corporate philosophy or blueprinting system, similar to the umbilical cord image of the spider plant.

Spider Plant Metaphor

The organizing of new structures in a CAS is illustrated by Gareth Morgan's (1997) metaphor of a spider plant. NASA found it to be the most efficient and adaptable plant for purifying the air on board a space station because of its self-organizing properties. Spider plants are commonly found in hanging baskets. There is a central plant in the basket, rooted in soil. From the basket, the plants send out long stems a foot or so in length. These stems act as tentacles. At the end of each tentacle are clumps of leaves that look like miniatures of the parent spider plant. The growth of a spider plant is not planned or controlled. It grows by self-organization. When it reaches a point where resources are available, it is ready to throw off a new shoot. The shoot itself grows through self-organization. The process goes on and on until the structure of the whole is very sophisticated and very complex. All of this occurs without centralized control or planning.

Focus on Actions

Embracing a nonlinear perspective when appropriate lets the change agent focus on the *actions* in the system, not the end points. Seeing the organization as a whole with all of its multiple interactions shifts the focus from organizational charts and strategic plans. Trying to shape events to accomplish explicit goals or fitting interactions into an organizational chart is not as important as responding to situations or rewarding initiatives that help the organization evolve. The following two examples illustrate how using a short list of "rules" or guiding principles has allowed two different organizations to focus on actions and to flourish.

Guiding Principles at VISA

Dee Hock (1998) lists the action perspectives and organizing principles that led to the creation of VISA:

- Participation must be open to all relevant and affected parties. (Membership establishes a *container* for self-organization.)

- Power and function must be distributed to the maximum degree. (By minimizing power differences, other *significant differences* can emerge.)

- Decisions must be made by bodies and methods representing all parties, yet dominated by none. (A *container* is established to distribute power across the system.)

- The company must seamlessly, harmoniously blend both cooperation and competition. (The *transforming exchanges* support multiple relationships among agents.)

- The company must be durable in purpose and principle while infinitely malleable in form and function. (*Container* is strong but flexible.)

- The company must release the human spirit and human ingenuity. (Transforming exchanges bring out human potential.)

As the VISA organization went past $100 billion in annual volume of transactions, it was coordinated by fewer than five hundred people, who created the prototype of their present communications system in ninety days for less than $30,000. Hock (1998) concludes that, given the right principles, quite ordinary people consistently do extraordinary things.

Simple Rules at Mercedes-Benz Credit

Petzinger (1999) relates the story of how Mercedes-Benz Credit CEO George Bauer realized the organization needed to cut costs and improve service to be more competitive, but he had no idea what might work. Employees would have to invent it themselves through trial and error. By keeping what worked, a new organization would emerge. Bauer wanted the employees to find the weaknesses in the organization—let it grow from the bottom up. The rules were few but firm:

- Attack service issues in teams;
- Cut costs;
- Every job, every procedure is fair game for change; and
- No fear.

Bauer promised that no one would be laid off no matter how much efficiency was introduced because he was confident he could grow the company. He said, "If you eliminate your job, you will be rewarded with another one."

The results? The company assets increased and they ranked first in their industry in customer satisfaction.

Structuring by Chunking

When an organization has decentralized into semi-autonomous units to take advantage of the speed of self-organization, it needs a means of managing these multiple containers. Creating changes and common purpose among the small containers without slowing down the process of adaptation requires a high degree of interrelationship among the units. Transforming exchanges among the parts provides this system-wide communication.

The concept of "chunking" is helpful here. Chunking in this sense refers to the phenomenon of complex systems emerging out of the links among simple systems that work well and are capable of operating independently. Chunking encourages the change agent to start small and experiment to find pieces that work and then link the pieces together. For example, the Internet evolved in chunks, with components being integrated into the system only after they had been individually refined, proven, and accepted by a collective jury.

We see the importance of relationships in high-performing teams in sports and in business. When teams are functioning well, we often look for ways to help the teams to work together and involve others. Connecting teams may result in a fundamentally new system that may need new group rules or procedures, again requiring leaders to adapt to unexpected outcomes in a CAS.

Change Agent Role

The unpredictability of the CAS has profound implications for the work of an organization change agent. The consultant must deal with change in the absence of clear, predictable goals or structures.

Table 4.1. Role of the Change Agent

	Emerging Goals, Plans, and Structures		
Phase	**Focus**	**Action**	**Outcome**
Contracting	Agents at all levels	If clients have clear end points or targets in mind, ask questions and provide examples of other CASs where end points emerged or shifted	Clients understand that end points can significantly shift as work progresses
Assessing	All levels	Make assessment that is just "good enough" to start; if delayed, the problem may shift	Work begins with salient issues
Intervening	All levels	Help establish short lists of simple rules that can shape coherent self-organization	Clients develop tools for continuing emergence
Evaluating	Because end points are not predictable, outcomes are not reliable as measures	Perform iterative evaluations with relatively short timelines	Learning and self-correcting system

Summary

In a CAS, vision, plans, structures, and controls emerge from the interaction of the system agents. The change agent supports action and experimentation, rather than focusing on arbitrary end points.

▶ METHOD: SELF-ORGANIZING EXERCISE

Purpose

We learned about this method first from Kevin Dooley. He uses it to help a group experience the dynamics of self-organization. We have taken many different groups through the process during team-building sessions and find that it opens a wide range of questions about the affective, cognitive, and physical dimensions of emergence. It becomes a wonderful metaphor to talk about self-organizing systems in organizations.

Preparation

This exercise requires a large open space in which participants can move around freely. We have done the exercise with as few as ten and as many as eighty. No explanation or set-up instructions are required.

Process

Participants distribute themselves throughout the space and stand so that they do not touch each other when their arms are extended.

The facilitator asks participants to relax and close their eyes. The facilitator encourages them to focus on their heads (what they are thinking) and their bellies (what they are feeling) in the course of the exercise.

Each participant selects a number between one and one hundred. The task of the group members is to arrange themselves in ascending numerical order in a circle. The rules for the interaction are posted:

· Keep eyes closed.

· Speak to only one person at a time, and only when you are touching the person to whom you speak.

After everyone understands the directions, the facilitator says, "Go." It is critical that the facilitator not intervene in any way during the exercise.

Participants will usually break the rules at some point and will generally become confused, but the facilitator should remain silent and observant. There should be no intervention until the group believes itself to be arranged in the circle. This usually takes between five and fifteen minutes.

When the group is silent or makes other indications that it is ready, the facilitator identifies the person with the lowest number and asks the remaining group members to count off as they go around the rest of the circle.

Debriefing

In discussing the activity with a group, the change facilitator should ask the following questions:

- Who thought the group would succeed? Why?

- Who thought the group would not succeed? Why?

- What were you feeling? How did your feelings change as you went through the process?

- What were you thinking? How did your thoughts and strategies change as you went through the process?

- Which rules did you break? At what point and why did you decide to break the rules?

- What were the container, significant differences, and transforming exchanges that allowed the group to self-organize?

- How would the self-organization have been altered with different container, significant differences, and transforming exchanges?

- How is this process similar to and different from organization change processes?

- What is the role and responsibility of the leader in such a situation?

- What would it mean to "manage change" in such a situation?

Applications

We have used this strategy to teach groups about self-organizing processes and the conditions that shape them, but we have also used it as a simulation to instigate organizational interventions. Three examples will demonstrate the power of the exercise.

Who's in Charge?

An intact work group called us in to help them deal with unsatisfactory communications. During the self-organizing exercise, the manager of the group moved immediately to the center of the circle. One by one his employees came to him. He listened to their numbers and told them where to go. This command-and-control strategy worked for about three minutes. Then the manager lost his orientation and began sending people to the wrong positions. As they realized what was happening, the employees started to laugh, but no one went to the manager to set him straight. Within minutes, the manager was so frustrated he opened his eyes and said, "This is what always happens. They laugh behind my back, and I never know why!"

The ensuing conversation about limits of a manager's omniscience in an organization led the group to consider new ways to work as interdependent agents in a self-organizing system.

Stretching the Rules

An international financial services company was facing massive issues with intercultural communications and securities violations. They called us for help. During the self-organizing exercise, one young man spoke to the group. He said, "Did she say we had to keep our numbers? If not, just stay where you are and count off in order." He began with "one." Two, three, and four fell in line. The person who would have been number five hesitated. She objected to the arbitrary changing of the rules, but others in the circle convinced her to "play along." Most were proud of their clever solution to the problem, but a few participants voiced their discomfort.

In the debriefing, the dissenters talked about rules and interpretation of rules and peer pressure to bend rules. This discussion led to a careful consideration of ethics in business, shared responsibility for ethical decision making, and respectful approaches to dealing with minority voices.

Planning for a Change

A high-tech organization was moving from a product development stage into production and distribution. The organization knew a change was coming and that it would have to transform itself quickly or lose market potential. We worked with organization members to plan the change effort. They used the self-organizing exercise as a simulation of rapid and distributed change. They talked about the containers, transforming exchanges, and significant differences that shaped the exercise. Then they used the model to define what conditions they needed to put in place to guide their process of self-organization into new business activities.

These are just a few of the insightful conversations that have emerged from applications of the self-organizing exercise. Every group sees in the experience the seeds of its own organizational dilemmas. The exercise and the debriefing conversation provide language and experiences that help frame new solutions to problems of emerging and open systems. ◄

The self-organizing exercise illustrates how goals, plans, and structures will emerge when the right conditions for self-organization exist: a good enough container, exchanges that transform the existing patterns, and significant differences between the agents. This latter condition is explored in depth in Chapter 5.

5

Amplify Difference (Not Build Consensus)

MANY ORGANIZATION CHANGE interventions (ranging from strategic planning to team building to large system transformation) focus on moving the organization to consensus. Divergent views, such as those derived from brainstorming in problem-solving activities, are encouraged early in the process. Ultimately, however, the group is moved to a decision or resolution that everyone is expected to support actively.

Too often, seeking consensus suppresses differences and generates solutions that lose the creativity and self-organizing potential of the group. A brainstormed list that picks out the commonality does not move self-organization forward. Picking out the differences will move the group beyond where it was (see Figure 5.1). Differences become generative, rather than merely a documentation of the consensus the group brought with them into the room.

Figure 5.1. Surfacing Differences

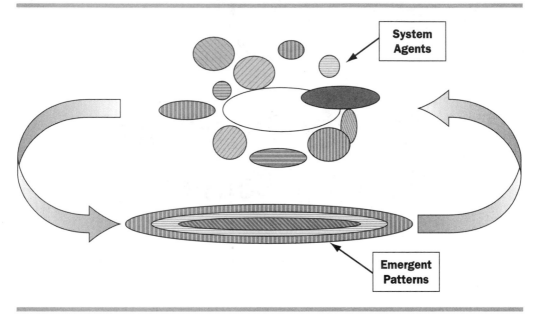

The pattern of a CAS reflects differences that have been integrated, not ignored or obliterated. Old patterns give way to new patterns in a continuous stream of self-organization. We recognize this succession of patterns as evolution of the system as a whole.

In this chapter we explore the dimensions of difference that are significant in a healthy CAS. Going beyond stereotypes, exploring hidden differences, raising the value of inclusion, and appreciating divergent perspectives and behavior are discussed.

In the following story, we see the consequences of suppressing important differences in organizations and what can happen to organizational patterns when a difference is finally acknowledged.

▶ STORY: THE HIDDEN DIFFERENCE

The consulting company, based in a small country, had prided itself on diversity. It had positioned itself to be a resource on diversity for its organizational clients. A diverse multinational team, which had worked successfully together for over a year, led the consulting group of sixteen. Team members had successfully surfaced and worked through their most obvious issue—race.

Shortly before a major marketing initiative, the four members of the executive committee were praised for their hard work in bringing the group together. In the midst of this celebratory moment, one of the committee members, Louise, announced her resignation. As a non-citizen, she was not permitted to hold certain jobs, a restriction that precluded her from positions of formal authority. Without this authority she could no longer provide leadership for the group. It was as if a bomb had been dropped. Everyone was shocked. Louise was recognized as their most capable consultant. The others valued her problem-solving skills, insightfulness, and decisiveness. How could this be? The formal chair of the group, Marcella, was very upset because Louise's comments felt like a personal attack on her leadership.

The bombshell that Louise dropped was a *hidden difference*—a difference that had not been acknowledged by the group, even though national origin was a big issue in the society. Louise was an American in a country in which local citizenship was required for certain jobs and standing in the community.

Everyone on the team knew about this issue, but the group had not discussed the impact of this "second-class" status on Louise. Unbeknownst to the group, the lack of status had been affecting Louise's ability to perform up to her potential. By the time the group was ready to move to the next phase of its work, expecting that Louise would continue to make her contribution, Louise had had enough of trying to provide leadership without sanctioned authority. The tight, coherent container created by the celebration of the group's success accentuated how differently Louise felt from the rest of the group. She became acutely aware of being an outsider.

Louise's resignation surfaced the important difference that had been unnoticed or disregarded by everyone but Louise. Members of the group may have wondered how she was coping with working in a new culture, but they assumed she was accepting the constraints.

The impact on the group was substantial at many levels. At the macro-level the group realized that part of its mission had to be to help non-citizen workers cope with the constraints. In the consulting group others began to step into leadership activities that by default had been undertaken by Louise. At the dyad level, Louise and Marcella had to repair a broken relationship. At the individual level, Louise wondered how she could make a contribution without formal authority, a position that did not suit her. ◀

Point of the Story

Every complex system includes an uncountable number of differences. Some are relevant to the work, and others are irrelevant. Some are explicit, and others are implicit in the group's interactions. Frequently, differences that are most divisive are the ones that are talked about least often. Other frequently avoided differences include race, socioeconomic status, and education level. Such unexamined differences build hidden fences that distort communication and interfere with the work of the group. Marshak and Katz (1999) describe the covert, questionable, illegitimate, and unacceptable processes that are "under the table" that block a group's effectiveness.

The Method: Difference Matrix, p. 95, is useful for a change agent to help a group see the positive consequences of dealing with their significant differences and the negative consequences of avoiding them.

An overzealous search for unity can bury significant differences. Hidden differences distort the interactions among system agents and interfere with effective self-organization. Effective change agents discover differences and use their power to promote positive change.

Unbraiding Differences

Individuals bring many differences to the workplace, including multiple group memberships. A person is a member of a family, neighborhood, religious and racial identity group. Individuals bring to the organization the knowledge they have gained from being in other complex systems. For example, family events affect the employee's functioning at work. When individual differences are recognized, valued, and amplified, they impact other aspects of the employee's life. For example, working in a foreign culture requires an understanding of the nuances in physical gestures and verbal communication. Working with differences helps people develop a more complex vocabulary. New metaphors develop. New solutions become apparent.

When differences are valued in this way, they are said to be "unbraided." As a rope can be unbraided, things that have been folded together into a single biased perspective can be taken apart. We go beyond the obvious physical characteristics that identify stereotypes. We are conditioned through life experience to seize on a physical difference, such as gender or race, and weave together a set of assumptions about what the person must be like. The generalization may be true for many, but it is a false characterization of any one individual.

By going beyond our associations and assumptions about gender or race, we unbraid the many aspects of a person and focus on less global differences. These differences are more likely to be associated with the behavior we perceive. Of course, each of the specific differences such as occupational background (for example, engineer, lawyer, farmer) can have its own set of stereotypes, but by exploring and understanding the other person we avoid the sweeping generalizations often bundled up with the most complex differences, such as gender and race.

Differences in a CAS

In a CAS, difference creates the impetus for change. It is the context that is necessary for adaptation. Just as electrical current requires a difference between positive and negative poles, just as difference in elevation makes water flow downhill, difference creates the potential for any change in the system.

Asymmetry allows for efficient growth and change. Mixed vegetation supports a stable ecosystem. Different gases burn in different colors and at different rates to ensure the fuel is used efficiently.

Organizations, too, thrive on difference. Specialization of function allows individuals to perform tasks at which they excel. Cultural differences introduce new perspectives and creative insights. Separate offices give employees an opportunity to express their individual tastes and introduce personal and family symbols into the workplace. Multiple hierarchical levels give explicit attention to the need to manage the whole as well as the parts of the organization.

Traditional organizational work focuses on building common ground or finding similarities in a group. Often this technique drives difference underground, where it continues to shape the patterns of behavior in unseen ways. By focusing on difference—articulating and obtaining agreement on differences that make a difference—an organization can bring forward and work intentionally with the patterns of interaction.

Goldstein (1994) discussed the critical importance of difference to adaptation. He cited a study of British string quartets and how the least successful were led by domineering first violins or by participatory democracy. The most successful quartet operated between these extremes, with an ambiguous, unresolved tension operating between the first violin and the rest of the group. The differences within the successful quartet were expressed and resolved, rather than dampened or ignored.

On a macro-scale, unresolved differences lead to organizational civil wars. Automobile makers' neglect of the safety issues raised by Ralph Nader in the 1960s had a huge impact. Ignoring the complaints of discrimination in companies has led to substantial financial losses and public embarrassment. Computer companies that disregarded the possibilities of the personal computer suffered major setbacks. In all of these cases, unrecognized difference disrupted organizational life and welfare.

Differences and Organization Resilience

Although difference introduces a potential for conflict, it also provides a rich repertoire of options. When an organization encounters a need for change, variations within its membership provide multiple ways to understand and respond.

IBM provides a powerful example of the dangers of homogeneity (Garr, 1999). In the 1970s and early 1980s, "Big Blue" was the paradigm of a well-oiled machine. It provided classes to new recruits to teach the IBM way to dress, behave, engage with clients, and deal with managers and peers. This focus on uniformity served the organization well while its market and technologies were relatively stable. When the computer world began to change, however, IBM was unprepared. Efforts to increase creativity and diversity within the company were unsuccessful. At one point, the company stretched its bounds to build relationships with the heterogeneous, creative, and unstructured corporate culture of Apple. Neither organization was able to overcome the large-scale conflict that followed, and the tentative joint ventures were abandoned.

Even the U.S. military recognized in the late 1980s the need to build internal diversity for the unpredictable challenges of the future. Their advertising jingle, "Be all you can be," signaled the end of the strictly controlled single vision of a person in uniform.

Healthcare professionals and their organizations have also recognized the more flexible and resilient responses of diversity. Nurses shed their starched whites and symbolic caps for more varied and patient-friendly garb. When they interact with patients, they provide more adaptive responses and are perceived to be more flexible and personally caring.

When integrated into a pattern of individual and group responsiveness, diversity and standards of professional disciplines increase the capacity for adaptation. In rapidly changing business and technical environments, the capacity to adapt becomes an indicator of success.

Differences and Organization Change

Clearly, there is great value in surfacing hidden differences. In the short run, whatever blocks organization functioning is removed. In the long term, the new interactions of agents in the group or organization lead to more adaptive patterns. The CAS focus on difference generates three major implications for a change agent: Amplification of communication, working toward greater inclusion, and supporting intermittence.

Amplifying Communication

Amplifying communications from clients helps the client to slow down the process and listen for understanding. As important differences among clients are revealed, the change agent must explore them to help the pattern to emerge.

When the group methods focus on difference, the discussion diverges and more options are identified. When differences have to be resolved, the group can decrease the container size, for example, form a fishbowl or charge a subgroup with the task of resolution. By contrast, nominal group techniques focus on similarity within the group. They lose the variety that is present and often end up with obvious or uninspiring cliches.

A dialogue about difference identifies the position of all parties to the issue. The self-organizing outcome is a new agreement for working together that draws from the talents and preferences of all in a process of mutual influence. The alternative is to collapse the rich potential of difference into a single explanation or expectation that keeps the organization in its current pattern.

Leaders can amplify the impact of people in the organization who are moving in a positive direction of change. By identifying and differentiating the people who are headed in a direction they favor, leaders can give them visibility and support. For example, Mary Ellen Heyde (2000), who was responsible for the Ford Windstar minivan, put a lot of women on the design and marketing teams because women were the primary customer base. They obtained input from customers who were mothers and created a "sleeping-baby mode" for the overhead light so that only the floor lighting turns on when the door is open.

Working for Inclusion

A certain amount of disorder and disruption are required for adaptation. The system must spend some time on an apparently random search for options before it discovers the most adaptive responses. If a system accepts only people who readily assimilate, the differentiation that is necessary for change and adaptation is reduced. The system becomes closed. It repels new ideas and perspectives. A CAS needs the disrupting influence of persons with different education and training, different experiences with the customers, and awareness of new markets.

In tightly controlled organizations, in which predictability and stability are prized, self-fulfilling prophecies eliminate the possibilities that come from difference. People who might "rock the boat" are kept under control. Organizations that value adaptation and change, on the other hand, see "trouble makers" as those who move the organization to its creative edge, where innovations are most likely to occur. In these organizations, the diversity of ideas and multiple perspectives bring about change. Traditional examples of organizations that value divergence in the ideas and work styles of their employees are advertising agencies, computer software firms, and toy companies.

The change agent can aid the process of inclusion of new entrants into the system by fostering positive, amplifying interactions between the new and current members of the system. Newcomers should be encouraged to express their concerns and ideas freely in their own unique ways. If free expression is not encouraged, the information and creativity of individuals with other life experiences may lie dormant.

Changing employee demographics provide a striking example of the need to integrate new and different perspectives. Generations of young workers are coming into corporate environments with new sets of expectations and values. Members of so-called "Generation X" see themselves as independent of and unrestricted by the traditions and mores of older generations. If new people are teased or put down, creativity is blocked by the immense pressure to conform.

Extreme differences or unconnected differences can generate frustration and impede productivity. Transforming exchanges, structured and encouraged by the organization and its change agents, can establish learning environments where the tension of difference provides a foundation for organization transformation.

Intermittency

Briggs and Peat (1990) describe a form of difference they call "intermittency"—sudden bursts of random behavior. Random behavior can serve as a transition from one state to another. In society, carnivals or fiestas are bursts of energy within social norms. Such celebrations seem to allow order to continue the rest of the year. Using a metaphor that describes the behavior of iron molecules after they are heated called "annealing," when degrees of freedom and number of possibilities are increased, a period of apparently random behavior ensues; but after the short disruption, things settle into a better place. Intermittency can result in renewal or transformation.

In organizations an irrational act or unfortunate incident can serve the purpose of intermittency. Such disruptions may stem from a managerial decision or some outside force (such as federal regulations). Regardless of the source, intermittencies challenge the normal order of business and focus attention on the weaknesses of standard routines. For example, the federal government challenge to Microsoft may ripple through the economy for years, as did the breakup of AT&T.

A change agent's role is to be attuned to the occurrence of these sudden bursts and inquire about the opportunities for learning. The change agent may provide an invaluable service in helping the system see the incident as a wake-up call. In the fields of OD and archetypal psychology, the trickster archetype is a source of intermittence. By acting as a trickster, the change agent provokes the system and stirs up energy for transformation.

Change Agent Role

The role of the change agent (shown in Table 5.1) is to help the group members be conscious of containers, surface and understand the differences that drive their interactions, and to establish transforming exchanges that allow the difference to generate learning. When the energy of the group is focused on differences that are unarticulated or irrelevant, the group's efforts may actually interfere with productive self-organization. When the group focuses its energies on differences that can

WHEN THE GROUP focuses its energies on differences that can make a significant difference, the work self-organizes into more productive patterns.

make a significant difference, the work self-organizes into more productive patterns. If productive patterns do not occur, then the difference addressed was not significant. For example, a consultant highlighted the age differences in a group that was unproductive, but nothing happened. When the disciplinary differences in the group were identified, the group self-organized to better utilize the skills of its members.

A change agent can help clients deal with competing beliefs and strong emotions without blowups by changing the container, for example, by shifting the focus from staff needs to customer needs.

Table 5.1. Role of the Change Agent

Amplify Differences			
Phase	**Focus**	**Action**	**Outcome**
Contracting	Obvious and sanctioned differences, such as authority, power, conflicts	Acknowledge and work within the identified differences	Consider that a different set of differences is shaping the group interactions and problems
Assessing	Hidden differences that would aid adaptive self-organization	Ask group "How are you different from one another?"	Group surfaces important differences
Intervening	Transforming exchanges	Set up training, mentoring, agreements, role negotiation	Differences shape the emerging pattern
Evaluating	Effects of dealing with the hidden difference	Determine whether evaluation criteria are relevant	Evaluation evolves during course of intervention

Summary

Difference is a resource for change in a complex adaptive organization. It provides the variety and energy that allow for transformation of individuals, processes, groups, and organizations.

Traditional organizational interventions, which focus on building common ground, undervalue the power of diversity to disrupt (if ignored) or generate (if integrated) organization change.

The role of the change agent is to help clients identify their significant differences, to establish transforming exchanges that will make the differences generative, and to articulate the self-organizing patterns that emerge.

► METHOD: DIFFERENCE MATRIX

Purpose

The Difference Matrix allows a group to analyze its own complex dynamics in terms of the degree of difference and the level of transforming exchanges among the system's agents.

Preparation

A group does not need to understand the basic dynamics of a CAS, but the change agent should explain the meaning of the differences that matter and the interactions across those differences that shape the behavior of a human system.

The Difference Matrix (Figure 5.2) represents four different dynamic patterns that emerge in self-organizing systems. Potential positive and negative outcomes are shown for each quadrant.

- *Quadrant 1:* High difference and many transforming exchanges is the domain in which self-organization is most likely to occur. In this quadrant, differences of perspective, data, or opinion are aired, and new insights are encouraged.

- *Quadrant 2:* Low difference and many transforming exchanges is the domain for sharing and caring about the same things. It is an exciting and rejuvenating experience, but too much time in this quadrant leads to low productivity.

- *Quadrant 3:* High difference and few transforming exchanges is the domain for building frustration and anger. Though it can be used to help a group avoid irrelevant conflicts, it also tends to increase the tendency of a CAS to split.

- *Quadrant 4:* Low difference and few transforming exchanges is the domain for rest and security. It includes basic values and unarticulated norms of behavior. Everyone agrees, and no one needs to talk. Though it provides security, it also can lead to entropy and death of the system because there is not sufficient difference to motivate progress.

Figure 5.2. Difference Matrix

	High Difference	**Low Difference**
Many Transforming Exchanges	**1** *Positive Outcomes* Learning Growth Self-organization *Negative Outcomes* Stress Conflict Exhaustion	**2** *Positive Outcomes* Celebration Reinforcement Energy *Negative Outcomes* Low productivity Wasted energy Factions
Few Transforming Exchanges	**3** *Positive Outcomes* Reflection Safety Clearing the decks *Negative Outcomes* Isolation Misunderstanding Frustration	**4** *Positive Outcomes* Comfort Belonging Rest and recovery *Negative Outcomes* Boredom Stagnation Death

No system stays in one or another of the quadrants for long, and different individuals are usually in different quadrants at the same time. The motion of a group through the quadrants can help a change agent see what next steps might be helpful to move a group into safe territory or into the rough and tumble world of Quadrant 1.

Process

There are many ways to use the Difference Matrix to support group reflection and decision making. We use it often to clarify the different needs of individuals in a group. The following process meets this goal.

1. Explain the parts of the Matrix.

2. Give participants a copy of the Matrix without words in each quadrant and ask them to think about which of the quadrants is most comfortable for them and why.

3. Ask each person to write the name of each of the other team members into the quadrants where they might be most comfortable.

4. Ask participants to share their own selected place and compare and contrast it with how others view their preferences.

5. Discuss how these different perceptions affect the working relationships and self-organizing dynamics of the group.

Debriefing

The Difference Matrix provides a safe approach to help groups identify their differences. Together they can decide which differences are significant, which are irrelevant, which support growth and learning in the group, and which block understanding and change. Usually when groups come together, they focus on their common ground, hoping to build a container that is strong enough to hold their work. Individual differences may be subverted through this process, and individuals may feel that they are not truly a part of the commonly defined whole. The Difference Matrix allows the group members to articulate both their similarities and their differences so that the individuals maintain unique identities, and the group as a whole has a stable foundation of commonality.

In discussing the activity with a group, the change agent should look for the following:

- Multiple differences that make a difference.

- Judgments about which quadrant is most productive for the work of the team and why.

- Common patterns of transition for the team. For example, many passive-aggressive groups tend to move from Quadrant 3 (when a boss is in the room) to Quadrant 2 (when they complain among themselves about the boss).

Application

This tool is helpful in a variety of contexts. We have used it in strategic planning sessions to help organizations compare and contrast their past, current, and future activities; to resolve issues of interpersonal conflict; and to articulate unproductive communication patterns between management and employees. One particular story will demonstrate how the Matrix can facilitate transforming conversations.

The Information Systems (IS) division of an international manufacturing company was at odds with itself. Its three major functions—new development, user support, and legacy system maintenance—were separated into three distinct departments. Conflicts among the three were traditional, but with increasing demand and decreasing resources, the friction was seriously interfering with the work of the division. We met with managers and supervisors of all three departments to develop a plan to improve communications and operations.

After explaining the structure and function of the Matrix, we asked each departmental team to identify issues it had with other departments and to place them on the Matrix. The groups presented their analyses to each other, and then they compared and contrasted their various perspectives.

During the conversation, three areas of greatest concern emerged. All three were located in Quadrant 3: high difference and few transforming exchanges. After "unbraiding" the differences, the group designed communication processes and tools that would move those issues into Quadrant 1. They left the two-hour meeting with new understanding and specific, but simple, action plans to improve the interactions of their groups. They took these actions:

- To improve informal communication, they decided to co-locate.

- To resolve management disagreements, they arranged a meeting among the three management teams to resolve issues that they could not resolve individually.

- To reduce the problems with jargon, each group made a glossary for the other two groups. This became a living document that they carried to meetings and modified as necessary.

Using the Matrix allowed these individuals to describe their differences and frustrations in an objective and rational context. They were able to relive and reinterpret difficult experiences, and thus they came to a better understanding of the differences among the groups. Their resulting plan of action was simple, but proved powerful in reducing friction and increasing productive working relationships across the organization. ◀

The Difference Matrix demonstrates how significant differences can be identified and amplified to foster self-organization. In Chapter 6 we discuss how these differences will foster change at all levels of the organization because of the self-similarity inherent in a CAS.

6

Self-Similarity (Not Differences Between Levels)

ORGANIZATION CHANGE works at different levels and places within the organization at the same time. The lead change agent coaches or conducts team-building sessions for top managers. Information specialists work with the chief information officer. A human resource consultant helps develop an employee assistance program. Although these various initiatives might be coordinated in some way, frequently they fail to use the inherent similarities in the issues and patterns that arise in various parts of the system.

If the organization were a machine, the interventions at various levels and functions, of necessity, would be distinct because machine parts do not influence each other in any way. In a CAS, however, the cycles of change create similar patterns at all levels of the system (see Figure 6.1). By focusing on the similar patterns, a change agent can bring coherence and full system change in more effective ways.

> **A CHANGE AGENT** who learns the simple rules that govern the behavior of a system on one level will have information to support decision making at other levels.

In this chapter we discuss the concepts of *self-similarity* (the phenomenon of similar patterns that occur at all levels of a CAS) and *scaling* (the variation of magnitude and frequency of these patterns). The "method" at the end of this chapter focuses on the *fractal* as a metaphor. Fractals can be used to illustrate the repetition of the same patterns of behaviors and creative differences in multiple places and times. A change agent who learns the simple rules that govern the behavior of a system on one level will have information to support decision making at other levels.

Figure 6.1. Similar Patterns Across Levels

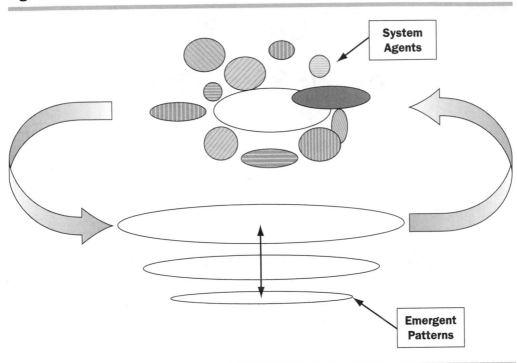

▶ STORY: THE HIDDEN DIFFERENCE (CONTINUED)

The case related in Chapter 5 is also useful here. Members of the group knew the hidden difference of nationality status. It was a major societal issue regularly debated in the legislature. It was the subject of numerous public policy debates and newspaper columns. Because the issue was very salient at the macro level, it is not surprising that it appeared at the micro level of a consulting organization. Yet this pattern was not acknowledged, and so the difference was not a part of the decision-making process for the organization.

The moral of the story is that change agents should attune themselves continually to multiple levels of the system and consider how those patterns appear in their environments. ◄

To help clients see the multiple levels and complex patterns of their issues, the Method: Fractal As Metaphor, p. 108, is helpful. Like an organizational Rorschach, this method helps groups explore interactions beyond the organization chart image.

Self-Similarity in Organizations

Living things are hierarchies of nested combinations. Atoms come together to form molecules. Molecules combine to form cells. Cells make up organs. Organs sustain the life of the creature. All of the parts are interconnected with semipermeable boundaries that enable free flow of information and resources. In an organization that functions as a CAS, each agent is nested in a combination of groupings and networks, all of which influence behavior. They are interdependent and complexly interactive (Wilber, 1998).

Any agent in a large organization is involved in a functional department (marketing, manufacturing, R&D), in a product division (computer chips, paper products), in market groups (teenagers, retired persons), and in the whole company. Through cross-training, computer intranets, and support staff, they are all connected. With some permeable boundaries, people can move from one unit to another. At any moment, each agent is positioned to learn more about the organization or about its external environment.

Ken Baskin (1998) describes how the self-similarity between departments in 3M helps them partner with customers with an "Integrated Solutions" program. By working with team members from marketing and R&D, salespeople map work flows for major customers and develop reports on how the customers can improve productivity and reduce costs. One customer was so impressed with the report and suggestions for improvement that they invited 3M to participate in their product design cycle. 3M, in effect, became part of this customer's operations.

Self-Similarity as DNA

The concept of self-similarity can be seen in DNA. In living things DNA is in all parts of the system. The information about the whole is encoded in all the parts. DNA is also changeable through evolutionary processes. This allows living systems to adapt to their environments.

When this metaphor is applied to organizations, we can see self-similarity in all departments and at all levels. So what works in one area probably has applicability in others. For example, successful innovations servicing customers in one Sears store will probably be valuable elsewhere. Managers can transfer their knowledge from one store to another. When these values and procedures are instilled, employees feel a sense of ownership, not just for their specialized jobs but also for how the whole company operates.

The corporate DNA does not explicitly dictate the behavior of the system agents because that behavior always has to be responsive to the local environment. The company's values and procedures give guidance about how to proceed, but it is the unique aspect in the specific circumstance that determines the specific response. Confronted by an angry customer, the company policy of "the customer is always right" is tempered with the agents' assessments of what is happening in the moment; the impact on nearby customers; and the intensity, duration, and likely outcome of the behavior. Agents self-organize as they sort out the conflicting messages of the corporate values, the behavior of other customers, and the details of their current situations (Baskin, 1998).

Scaling

Scaling distinguishes a random system from a complex adaptive one. *Scaling* is the tendency of a complex system to *repeat the same patterns* in many different parts of the system and at many different levels of magnitude and frequency. A random system has no complex similarities between behavior patterns in one part of a system and another part of the same system. Individual behavior is ruled by chance. A complex system will exhibit similar patterns across the system. A hierarchical pattern in structure is reflected in the culture, in the organization systems, and in the day-to-day behavior of its members (Chan Allen, 1998). Disney World is often cited as an example of a strong customer service culture. There is a great diversity of individual behaviors by the "cast members" because every interaction with a customer is unique, but because this system follows similar patterns, similarities across the system are recognizable. Customers are consistently satisfied.

Scaling in Organizations

Examples of scaling are easy to find in organizations. Dress, norms, habits, and traditions all emerge as patterns. Values are shared and reflected among individuals in different contexts within the same organization. Perspectives and standard operating procedures should also demonstrate the self-similarity between levels and across functional areas.

The importance of scaling for a change agent is the insight that a CAS always has some similarity at all levels of the system—individual, group, and organization-wide. A consultant can see many instances where this is so. Thus, learning about a system on one level provides information about all of the other levels.

For example, different departments in the same organization will share values, procedures, or communication habits. Individual employees adopt each other's forms of dress and behavior. Teams replicate the interpersonal norms of other teams. This self-similarity is explicit even in trivial situations. For example, you will seldom find an immaculate coffee area on one floor and a filthy one on another floor of the same company. The behavioral norms are self-similar across the organization.

Communication symbols, such as logos, company rituals, and stories bind an organization together by defining what all of the individuals share, in spite of the differences in their skills, talents, or organizational levels. The same patterns appear across all levels.

> WHEN CRITICAL characteristics are not scaled in the organization, for example, when a leader behaves in one way and expects different behavior from employees, dangerous rifts develop in the esprit de corps.

When critical characteristics are not scaled in the organization, for example, when a leader behaves in one way and expects different behavior from employees, dangerous rifts develop in the esprit de corps. Groups develop distrust and lose a sense of loyalty to an organization that disregards the need for scaled values and expectations.

Corporate identity and individual identities are frequently expressed as sets of scaled characteristics. When enough fundamental elements are shared by members of a corporate body, their sense of belonging is reinforced and they develop an identity based on what they all hold in common.

Corporate culture is also an outcome of scaled and shared characteristics. The culture emerges, not as a single, undifferentiated whole, but as a collection of behaviors or beliefs held in common. Over time, the scaled patterns take on a coherence in the organization that can be observed as the "culture" of the people and the place.

Organizational patterns, such as hierarchies, are also effects and causes of organizational scaling. Attitudes toward authority, behavioral norms, and performance expectations are replicated across an organization. If those patterns tend toward control and risk aversion, then a hierarchical structure will emerge. After the scaled pattern is complete, new activities and persons will be constrained to work within the pattern or find themselves excluded from the paths of communication and power.

Simple Rules

Self-similarity is facilitated by simple rules—the minimum set of guidelines or norms that circumscribe behavior in a system. If all of the agents in a system follow the same simple rules, then each one adapts to his or her immediate and local circumstances effectively, while remaining a part of the larger system. Each makes independent and adaptive responses, yet the system as a whole generates complicated patterns of coherent action. The classical example of the short list of simple rules is a flock of birds. Computer simulation models have demonstrated that flocking behavior can be explained simply. Three rules are sufficient to generate flocking behavior: (1) Match your speed to others'; (2) Do not run into others; and (3) Move toward the center. Each bird follows these rules, and the flock as a whole is able to move in a coherent fashion.

The foraging behavior of ants can be explained with a simple rule: "Keep foraging as long as incoming food is accepted by other ants in the colony."

Individuals experience the short list of simple rules when driving on a crowded highway. Their immediate actions are not guided by some system-wide understanding of traffic patterns, but by simple rules: Stay in my lane; leave two car lengths in front of me; match my speed to others.' These simple rules, in addition to longer range expectations based on the destination, allow drivers to participate safely in the system that we recognize as rush-hour traffic.

The implication for change agents is (1) to observe current rules and reflect these to the group/organization or (2) help the group/organization to establish a new set of rules they will want in the future. For example, a company we consulted with had competing parts that needed to collaborate. In an intergroup meeting, they developed the following rules for working together:

- Listen twice, speak once;
- Make expectations explicit; and
- Say "thank you."

Organization change does not need to flow from the management level. Change can emerge and take shape through evolution. With a general sense of the direction of the change, organization agents can build on ideas, actions, and events that result from group interactions.

For example, unlike its department store competitors that distribute long lists of rules and procedures to employees, Nordstrom hands out one card that says

"Rule #1: Use your own good judgment. There is no rule #2." As a result there is great variety in how personnel respond to situations. The department heads see themselves as running their own businesses and function like entrepreneurs. The structure and procedures for working are fluid but are able to organize around what needs to be done.

Change agents are also aware of the power of a few simple rules, such as those used in Owen's (1997) *Open Space Technology:*

- Everyone has a choice;

- Whoever comes are the right people;

- Whatever happens are the only things that matter;

- It starts and ends at the right time; and

- Honor the "Law of Two Feet" (Leave when you wish).

These simple rules support self-organizing structures of learning and action.

Change Agent Role

When a change agent uses the continuous cycles that are the natural life of a CAS, the energy of the system is turned toward transformation, not toward resistance to change. Often, organizations seem stuck in a culture and patterns of behavior that reflect the choices that the organization made for survival. The change agent can shift the focus to those elements that have the most potential for adaptation. Often that may be the mind-sets or mental models that embody a small set of rules that keep the system stuck. Developing a new set of rules or behavioral principles at all levels of the system will give the system the impetus and coherence for change.

Table 6.1. Role of the Change Agent

Self-Similarity			
Phase	**Focus**	**Action**	**Outcome**
Contracting	Nonlinear aspects of the system	Contract for iterative application of short list of rules	More varied, more valuable than linear process
Assessing	Short list of rules that drive behavior of system at all levels	Identify and find leverage points	Determine needed shifts in the short list of rules
Intervening	Rules to support self-organization	Articulate and implement new rules	System builds coherent patterns with local variation
Evaluating	Emerging purposes	Frequent and iterative evaluations	Adapt to meet needs of organization

Summary

The path of change in a CAS is not a straight line from past to future. Rather, it is a continuous process of iterative action. A simple process that can be applied in a wide variety of environments is a much more effective change strategy than a sophisticated list of goals, objectives, and timelines. The process allows the group to make change, not just to talk about it.

▶ METHOD: FRACTAL AS METAPHOR

Fractals

A *fractal* is a geometrical object that is generated by solving nonlinear equations iteratively and plotting the series of solutions. The resulting image is extremely intricate, varied, and beautiful. It includes diverse colors and shapes, but identifiable patterns are repeated across the image. The coherence does not stop there. A small piece of the image can be magnified thousands of times, and the same self-similar patterns will still be visible. The two fractal images[4] (Figure 6.2) that appear on the follow-

---

[4]For an elegant and clear description of what a fractal is and how it is generated, refer to *The Turbulent Mirror* by Briggs and Peat (1990), page 96.

ing pages are examples of the infinite variety of computer-generated fractal images. Many natural structures (leaves, chemical crystals, riverbeds, and spider plants) also exhibit fractal patterns.

The fractal demonstrates one of the identifying characteristics of a complex adaptive system. The same patterns of behavior or relationship appear in multiple places and times across the organization. Examples of fractal self-similarity are easy to find. Dress, norms, habits, and traditions or organizations all emerge as self-similar characteristics. Values are shared and reflected among individuals in different contexts in the same organization. Perspectives and standard operating procedures should also demonstrate the self-similarity between levels and across functional areas.

> **EXAMPLES OF** fractal self-similarity are easy to find. Dress, norms, habits, and traditions or organizations all emerge as self-similar characteristics.

Figure 6.2. Computer-Generated Fractal Patterns

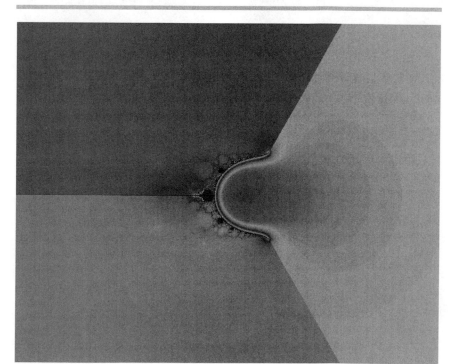

Figure 6.2. Computer-Generated Fractal Patterns, Cont'd

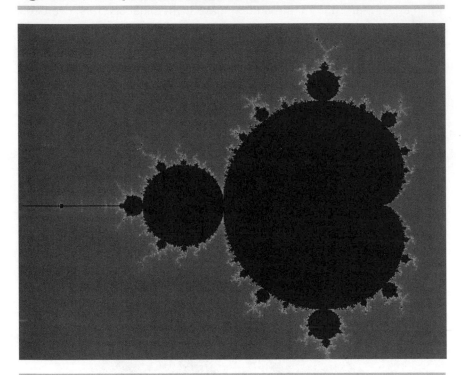

A fractal can be identified because it:

- Repeats the same patterns in different parts and in different levels of the object, for example, the angles between the veins in a leaf are the same as the angles between the twigs and roots of the same tree;

- Generates fuzzy boundaries, for example, the shore of a lake is jagged, no matter how far away you choose to observe it; and

- Encompasses areas of more and less stability, for example, the edge of a crystal can continue to grow, while the internal parts of it have already found stable structures and ended their growth and development.

All of these characteristics of fractals make them interesting metaphors for organization interactions and structures.

Purpose

This fractal exercise helps a change agent become aware of the current balance of the system. It sets the framework for amplifying difference or similarity to move toward more productive balance.

A CAS must balance similarity and difference. If there is only similarity, the system collapses because nothing energizes its behavior. If there is too much difference, the system shifts attention from one focal point to another. Agents move continually. They experience no respite or comfort. Everything remains in motion and expands until the system explodes. The healthy CAS balances self-similarity for coherence with difference for adaptation.

This activity uses fractal images to help a group reflect on its own complex patterns of behavior. We have found that a fractal image helps a group talk about its differences and self-similarities in new and insightful ways. It also provides a context in which group members can reflect on their relationships with one another and with other groups openly and dispassionately. In some instances, the fractal becomes the organizational Rorschach, helping people think about the dynamic interactions in their organizations that transcend the usual organization chart images.

Preparation

The change agent will need to obtain an image of a fractal that can be projected on a screen. Images can be downloaded or generated from packages that are available on the Internet. A web search for "fractal" will generate a large number of Internet sites. We will not provide URLs here because they change so often. New and exciting sites come online frequently. Some provide ready-made fractal images. Others allow the user to set parameters and generate unique fractal images.

Process

The change agent projects a fractal image onto a screen and asks the group a series of questions about how the image does and does not represent the group's experience and understanding of working in its own environments. An open discussion about the meaning of the fractal will generate perspectives and insights. A structured process can be used, as well, to focus the discussion and move it from self-organizing insight into controlled and structured work. Consider the following process.

1. Divide the group into subgroups who share some characteristic that is relevant to the issues (department, function, education, gender).

2. Ask each group to look at the same fractal image and identify ways that the patterns are similar to and different from their organizational interactions. The following questions will help elicit significant insights as a group considers the fractal as a metaphor for its organization:

   - How is this image similar to your experience and understanding of your organization?

   - What relationships do you see represented in this image, and how do they relate to the relationships in your organization?

   - Which parts of the image might represent your clients?

   - Which parts of the image might represent your leadership groups?

   - What can the fractal image tell you about the relationships between service providers and customers?

   - Which parts of the image and which parts of your organization are most stable? (Differences in perceived stability of parts of the organization show in the fractal as solid colors. Less stable parts will be mottled in color or shape.)

   - What can the image tell us about internal communications of the organization?

   - How might we take action to establish transforming exchanges that will make a more coherent image of our own organizational fractal?

   - What are the behavioral or belief patterns that are repeated across our organization?

   - What are the behavioral or belief differences that separate sections of our organizational fractal?

3. Have each group share its interpretation with the others.

4. Encourage the group, as a whole, to draw a new fractal image that represents the ways group members might wish to work together.

Debriefing

In discussing this activity with a group, the change agent should look for the following:

- Differences in interpretation of the fractal image among individuals and identifiable groups.

- Patterns of similar understanding among all group members.

- Recurring issues regarding patterns of organizational behavior.

- Options for increasing integration across existing boundaries.

- Possibilities of reframing organizational perceptions by shifting the interpretation of the fractal. For example, "What if this spot in the middle represented the client rather than the CEO? How would that affect our organizational effectiveness?"

Application: Large Membership Organization

A worldwide membership organization of eight million people was looking toward the next century and a transformation of its organizational structure and mission. A committee was formed that crossed international, philosophical, and organization lines. The committee expected to create a step-by-step model to move the organization into a more responsive and vibrant existence. After two years of work, the committee floundered. The members discovered that such a plan required infinite detail, and each detail became a source of dissention. After some months of struggling with a complicated plan for action, they were ready to give up. Frustration, exhaustion, and anger were the predominant patterns. They needed an alternative to the linear, pre-designed paths they were trying to create.

After a time of reflection and data collection, the committee began to investigate CAS approaches to planning and organization change. The concept of the fractal captured their collective imagination. They wanted the future of the organization to embody a pattern that would be recognizable from the individual, to the local, to the national and international organizational structures. They had a sense that their mission and the historical tradition might provide material for just such a fractal pattern.

The committee began to think about its work in terms of a short list of simple rules that would generate self-similar patterns across all levels of the organization. How might they establish a short list of rules that would move the organization forward in a diverse yet coherent direction?

They chose three rules:

· Listen to disparate voices from the community;

· Reflect carefully about the new information that emerges; and

· Recommend options that respond to the emerging patterns of the whole.

Rather than anticipating all of the plans and objections of the whole organization, the group began to use its simple rules. It listened, reflected, and recommended; then it began the cycle again. Individuals in their local environments completed the cycle. It was used to frame agendas for committee meetings. It was applied to select new members to join the committee. It became the basis for written documents, presentations, and data collection and analysis. Soon, cycles of transformation were occurring throughout the organization.

Individuals were transformed as they learned from one another. The committee was rejuvenated as it turned its attention to growth and adaptation, rather than to details of implementation.

The committee found that this approach provided opportunities for effective action, without demanding agreement on every detail. The resulting mission and structure could be implemented in an infinite number of ways in a wide variety of circumstances. Each person in each location and in all levels of the organizational hierarchy was able to live the mission of the organization in a way that reflected his or her gifts and the needs of the environment. Like a fractal image, many iterations of the simple rules generated a highly complex but coherent whole. ◄

The fractal method illustrates the phenomenon of self-similarity throughout a CAS and how a few simple rules explain complex interactions. Some behavior and interactions have more impact on organization change because they fit with the needs of the environment, as we explain in Chapter 7.

7

Success As Fit with the Environment (Not Closing the Gap with an Ideal)

MUCH ORGANIZATION CHANGE WORK is based on an assessment of the present state of the organization compared to an ideal future state. Change agents assume that the gap between the present and future states provides energy for movement toward the ideal. Sometimes this process is successful, but frequently the future is easier to imagine than to create. When a preferred future is defined for the whole organization, individual members find it difficult or impossible to take actions that will move toward the goal. Unless the vision of the future is grounded in current reality, it will not be helpful. Vision statements that are disconnected from current reality create a gap that is too large to cross. Complicated sets of goals and objectives become ends in themselves, so they fail to bridge the gap.

CAS offers an alternative. Agents, in the context of the whole, define their *local* aspirations and take *local* action to close *local* gaps. This pattern of individual action in immediate contexts is defined as "fit with the environment."

In a CAS, as we see in Figure 7.1, agents move toward a pattern that is a good fit for their needs and that aligns with opportunities in the environment.

Figure 7.1. Establishing Fit with the Environment

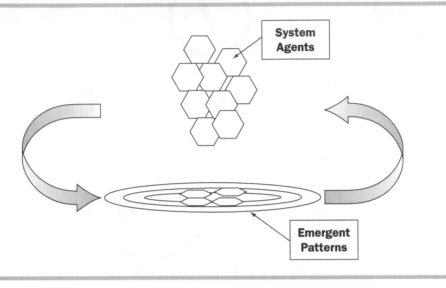

The following story shows the problem of preparing a strategy to close a gap and how an adaptive approach works better in a CAS.

▶ STORY: FOCUSING ON FIT

A suburban Chicago bank wanted to improve the quality and cost-effectiveness of its customer services. A management-planning group came together to set performance goals and institute a process to meet those goals.

The group's initial view was a traditional one in which they planned to (1) identify the preferred future state and (2) make plans to close the gap between the present and the proposed future. The planning team members ran into three problems with this strategy. First, their vision of the ideal bank was so different from the current one that it was difficult to imagine a bridge from one to the other. Second, they could not agree on the amount of detail or specificity that was required for the vision of the future. Some were happy with a single scenario, given from the customers' point of view. Others wanted detailed outcomes related to every aspect of the envisioned reality. Third, the planning group was accountable to many different external and internal customers, including small businesses, big businesses, wage earners, families, retail companies, startup companies, investors, staff and employees, and community business partners. None of these customers shared the same vision of the imagined future.

All of these difficulties turned the simple objective of "closing the gap" into an insurmountable challenge. The members of the planning group began to look for other ways to meet the challenge to improve services, and they hit on a different definition of success—fit. They decided that their present and future customer services included many different interactions and interfaces. They saw that each meeting point between a lender and a customer represented a possibility for improvement.

If every interaction optimized the "fit" between the bank lender and the customer, then service would be improved, and resources would be conserved. They realized that they would not be able to predict specific outcomes, and they would lose immediate control of the shape of customer service. They also realized that every member of the bank could contribute energy to the transformation of the whole if he or she were given the latitude to evaluate what it meant to "fit" within the bank's mission and to take action within bounds to accomplish an optimal fit. Bit by bit, decision by decision, and action by action, the pattern of customer service was transformed.

Each of the senior vice presidents was accountable for developing his or her own niche. The vice presidents were encouraged to "do their own thing" and pursue areas that would be profitable to them and to the bank as a whole. Over a period of several years, niches were developed in such specialized areas as an East Indian business community, small business administration, lending, and equipment leasing. The bank moved into a future that was very productive, as the whole system self-organized into a more efficient and effective pattern that fit the environment. ◀

Point of the Story

The "gap" approach to change depends on an unreliable description of a preferred future state. If the environment is stable and predictable, an organization vision may give a basis for action. If the future is uncertain, then the gap between present and future cannot provide insights for change. Fitness focuses on the gap between two present situations, both of which can be known. By focusing on fitness, change emerges from interactions, rather than depending on pre-determined detailed designs.

In this chapter we discuss the concept of fitness and fitness landscapes applied in organizations. Behaviors to increase fitness in two areas of application are discussed: performance feedback and balancing cooperation and competition.

A useful method to test for fitness is Method: Same and Different, p. 126. A group is able to identify significant differences and make a time-limited plan for resolving the difference.

Success As Fitness

The organizational world thrives on metaphors of winning, often borrowing images from the sports world, where competition and winning is everything. The scientific justification for the notions of natural selection and fitness stem from traditional understanding of Darwin's concept of survival of the fittest.

In nature, fitness measures include survival and reproduction under conditions of intense competition (Clippinger, 1999). An organism is fit if its adaptation has prepared it to work productively in an ever-changing environment, just as a jazz ensemble playing outdoors in Disneyland has to adapt continuously to the response of the changing crowds.

In a CAS, being fit does not necessarily mean beating the competition, accomplishing a goal, or winning the race. All of these metaphors imply an end to the process and no need for further adaptation. As we say in Chapter 4, there is no end point in a CAS. "Fit" in a self-organizing process becomes a dance in which agents shift continuously in concert with an ever-changing environment.

Fitness Landscape

Researchers use the concept of fitness landscapes (Kauffman, 1993, 1995) to explain the kind of behaviors that lead to success in nature. A fitness landscape is used as a metaphor for the environment in which the agent learns and takes action. In the process, both the agent and the environment are transformed. This mutual transformation is sometimes referred to as co-evolution.

The concept of co-evolution acknowledges that both the environment and the individual agents change to match each other. In nature species co-evolve as one discovers a new innovation and uses new parts of the landscape, for example, a new food source. This alters the fitness landscape for all the others, for example, an area vacated becomes an area of opportunity for other species.

In an organization, each new decision shifts people's positions on the landscape. When new levels of achievement are reached (a new peak is climbed), this sets new standards for the competition. In the meantime, decisions that others are making and changes in the environment shift the shapes of the fitness hills and valleys. On such an ever-changing landscape, the path toward success involves continuing vigilance. Every decision must be assessed in terms of an understanding of the past and reliable perceptions of the future.

> **SUCCESS MAY NOT be measured by reaching the highest peak, but by making the right move on the landscape at the right time to increase adaptation. In an organization, fitness is measured by sustainability over time under adverse conditions.**

These understandings and perceptions lead system agents to adapt to rugged landscapes by making changes in the local area that improve their positions the most. Success may not be measured by reaching the highest peak, but by making the right move on the landscape at the right time to increase adaptation. In an organization, fitness is measured by sustainability over time under adverse conditions.

Some businesses have developed co-evolving processes that go beyond traditional collaboration (Eisenhardt & Galunic, 2000). Because the objectives of collaboration are efficiency and economies of scale, typically the collaborative relationships remain static. A co-evolving process has growth and agility as its objective; consequently, the links among the businesses are always evolving.

Organizational Fitness

What are the organizational behaviors required to reach a desirable future? By acting on the possibilities in the present time, the future of the system is generated.

The drive to act comes from within in response to the excitement of the present significant differences, not by scrambling to reach some "stretch" goal. World-class baseball players do not set out to bat 1000. They work to know the history of the pitchers and the mechanics of their stances, and train their eyes to see the ball on its release from the pitcher. Many other variables affect the moment of hitting the ball. With diligent attention to these issues, the batting average takes care of itself.

To remain poised at a high level of performance, agents must continually improvise. They must avoid the extremes of too much or too little structure. Staying in the space between rigidity and randomness yields resilient, adaptive behaviors as iterative agent interactions produce productive patterns.

Transforming exchanges are absolutely necessary to this process. The only way to know whether an action was successful is to collect information about the consequences of that action. The only way to know the consequences is to collect information through a complex network of transformative exchanges, to analyze that information, and to use it to plan the next step on the path toward fitness.

To navigate the landscape, a human organization must have flexibility, that is, the ability to reproduce what has been successful in the past while responding to new opportunities in its environment. In a complex environment, an organization must be open to learning new strategies continuously. Its system of control has to be distributed throughout the organization, not lodged in a single leader or hierarchy. Organizations with agents who are scanning the environment are more able to process signals from their environments. An example cited by Roos (1997) is the manufacturing firm Sencorp, where the top management team describes its corporate identity as "the emergent behavior of knowledgeable organizational members." The strategic plans and direction in Sencorp result from the interaction and decisions of its members as they respond to marketplace opportunities. They are not dependent on a direction imposed from the top.

Importance of History

Finding one's way in the fitness landscape is not just about climbing new peaks or pursuing the latest fad, hoping for short-term results. Most successful companies continuously remind themselves of their histories and their origins to remember what the business is about. A firm anchor in an organization's history helps keep the focus on the long term.

Petzinger (1999) tells the story of the Avedis Zildjian Company, a family business that is the oldest business operating in the United States. Their business is drum making for "speakeasy drummers who invented jazz, for Ringo Starr and the Boston Symphony and thousand of marching bands in America." In the late 1970s, when there was not a family member who had studied drums ready to take over the business, management of the company was turned over to "professional outsiders" who focused on cutting costs and improving the quarterly results. Two factors in the company's past success—its renowned product development efforts and its close relationship with the drumming community—were neglected. The front office lost its connection with the essence of the product and the company hit hard times.

The family member in charge finally realized what was happening and in the mid-1990s recruited a new CEO who "cared about music." The new CEO was a longtime bass guitarist who had also been a senior executive in a food manufacturing company. He began taking drum lessons, strengthened the Artists Relations

Department, and started a new R&D team. The company also persuaded Ringo to visit the plant. A studio was set up in the middle of the headquarters building for visiting drummers. The visitors tested new drums where employees could regularly hear them. Playing drums during lunch breaks was encouraged for all employees.

In other words, the company went to its history to help find the corrective actions it needed to regain a fit with the drumming community.

Performance Feedback

In organizations, one of the rituals that relates to fitness is performance feedback, when individuals receive information about how they are fitting in with the environment.

The problem with performance feedback from a complexity perspective is that performance management systems are supported by a mechanistic view of organizational behavior. It is not possible to relate evaluation of employees to predetermined goals in a CAS, because the system is not predictable and the environ-

IT IS NOT POSSIBLE to relate evaluation of employees to predetermined goals in a CAS, because the system is not predictable and the environment is unstable.

ment is unstable. Effective performance appraisals should relate to how well the employee fits the needs of the organization and its stakeholders. Meaningful and productive employee behavior is too variable and emergent for the leader to understand or evaluate in detail. Trying to connect behavior to goals that are no longer relevant puts employees in a bind. They must ask themselves, "Should I do what I know is important, or should I do what will get me a good performance appraisal?" In such a context, leaders need new alternatives for performance feedback. We suggest the following:

- Avoid rigid goals that block the conversation and limit adaptation to new opportunities. Feedback can focus on performance, but goals can emerge from the interaction. Focusing too much on achieving goals diminishes the receiver of the feedback.

- Agents need positive feedback that amplifies their behavior, but they also need critical feedback that sets and maintains limits. Seeing a balance between the pluses and minuses allows the individual to transform.

- The feedback must be mutual, trusting that both the giver and receiver will make sense of what emerges. Clarity is something to be discovered during the feedback process; it is not pre-ordained.

- Feedback givers should not pretend that they have no personal interest in the results. This stance interferes with a mutual relationship. The person giving feedback must disclose his or her motives as they become pertinent.

- The receiver may be interested in the full range of the giver's observations, feelings, and values. If the giver controls the dialogue by pruning whatever could be offensive, it tends to dehumanize the exchange.

- One outcome of a feedback session should be increased fit with the organizational mission and the environment.

From a complexity perspective, the purpose of feedback is to establish transforming exchanges that are productive. When feedback generates questions, rather than provides answers, a two-way transforming exchange is more likely to occur. Even questions that seem negative may produce self-organization, new learning for both parties, and new bases for the emerging relationship.

The cycle times for feedback loops should be varied, according to the contents and contexts of their messages. A combination of short-, medium-, and long-term feedback loops provide cohesion and coherence to an otherwise unstable system. For example, a manager might give some messages in immediate one-on-one interactions. Other messages are appropriate for regular weekly meetings. Still others should be saved for quarterly or annual gatherings.

An infinite variety of transforming exchanges provides the glue to hold the complex, dynamic system together in the midst of continual change.

Competition and Cooperation

Fitness implies a relationship between an agent and its environment. In this engagement there can either be *competition, cooperation, or a mixture of the two.*

The concept of "Social Darwinism" has historically been used to justify ruthless competition and the use of any means necessary to attain profit goals, occupy new land, and so on. The assumptions are that what is subsumed must have been flawed and that the survivor is somehow superior.

Competition implies a contest between self and other—a struggle in which the fittest "wins." Although competition is necessary in nature to sort out the efficient from the inefficient, cooperation is also an important survival characteristic. In a healthy CAS, both competition and cooperation are necessary for sustainability.

Species do not adapt by wiping out other species. They survive by finding a niche on the fitness landscape. By so doing they leave a niche open in which others survive and prosper. In effect, they increase their own and others' chances for survival by being creative and adapting to the environment.

For example, shore birds with varying beak lengths have learned to "cooperate" in seeking out the territory appropriate to their beak lengths. The short-beaked birds search for food in the sand and rocks at the water line. The medium beaked birds wade out a few feet to get the snails just under the water line. The longer beaked birds wade out into deeper water to catch the small fish. In this way the differences among the species fit with the differences in the environment, so the system as a whole thrives.

Tit for Tat

The paradox of competition-cooperation is demonstrated by the "tit-for-tat" strategy discovered by Robert Axelrod (1997), a political scientist, who tested competitive strategies using computer simulations. Using Anatol Rapport's "tit-for-tat" program, Axelrod discovered that the most successful contestants started by cooperating on the first move and then doing exactly what the other contestant had done on the previous move. The strategy was "soft" in the sense that the person always used a cooperative pattern first. It was "hard" in that the person punished the opponent's uncooperative behavior by competing on the next move. The person returned to cooperation (forgiving) once the other party demonstrated the same. The strategy was consistent in that the other person could figure out exactly what would happen next. Axelrod has used this simple strategy to understand many complex adaptive systems: trench warfare during World War I, politics, and fungus growth on rocks.

The phenomenon of cooperation-competition is a fundamental part of the VISA system. Member institutions and banks that issue VISA cards compete vigorously for the same pool of customers, but they also cooperate. The systems works only because merchants and vendors accept any card anywhere in the world, without regard for who issued it. Dee Hock, who founded the VISA organization, says, "Neither competition nor cooperation can rise to its highest potential unless both are seamlessly blended. Either without the other swiftly becomes dangerous and destructive" (Waldrop, 1996, p.8).

The combination of competition and cooperation has also fostered the growth of a global system that operates without the traditional constraints of culture, language, currencies, or political systems. A complex system with multiple dimensions permits cooperation on some dimensions and competition on others. It is the multidimensional nature of complex systems that allows competition and cooperation to co-exist.

Collaboration and Competition

The implication of the tit-for-tat strategy for organization change is that change agents can coach leaders in how to cooperate, but also in how to be a skillful competitor when necessary. Leaders may be cooperative and competitive at the *same time* on *different dimensions*. For example, a department head may cooperate with other departments in designing new processes, while competing for funds in the budget cycle. In terms of the Thomas-Kilmann (1974) Conflict Mode Instrument, the assertive strategies of both competition and collaboration are essential. Contrary to recent popular theories of leadership, a positive, always-cooperative leader could easily be put out of the game. The always-competitive leader would also soon find himself or herself left out as others form alliances and cooperatives.

Change Agent Role

When success is defined as fitness, many options are possible. Some are rejected and others survive to be propagated to other parts of the system. Everyone learns from his or her own experiences and those of others in an iterative process. Change agents and leaders are essential to keep the concept of organizational fitness in the forefront.

Table 7.1. Role of the Change Agent

Success As Fitness			
Phase	**Focus**	**Action**	**Outcome**
Contracting	All levels of the system	Contract to provide capacities and perspectives to move client to greater fit with the environment	Client more open to adaptation and fit

Table 7.1. Role of the Change Agent, Cont'd

	Success As Fitness		
Phase	**Focus**	**Action**	**Outcome**
Assessing	Are external and internal feedback loops sufficient to support transforming exchanges?	Evaluate current significant difference, exchanges, and containers for their capacity to support self-organization	Help frame the interventions that will help establish better conditions for self-organization
Intervening	Building capacity to collect and respond to information	Use tit-for-tat strategy with client. When the clients help themselves, then the change agents help; when client stops, the change agent stops.	This leaves the responsibility for action and change with the client, where it belongs
Evaluating	Fitness, based on information across many boundaries	Measure how quickly the organization responds to external or internal changes	Focuses group on searching for fitness

Summary

Gaps—differences between the present and a preferred future—move a system to action. If those gaps are defined at a system-wide level, however, individuals have difficulty identifying their roles in the change. In a CAS, the focus for change is at the individual, local level. Each system agent tries to close the gap between itself and its environment. The process is called building fitness, and the outcome is success of the complex system and its agents.

Change agents can support this process in a variety of ways. They can help the organization to focus on its history and mission, teach and demonstrate effective methods of providing feedback, and help clients blend their needs for cooperation and control.

When a system focuses its energy on specific differences, it can generate new options for action. This continual process of improvement increases the fitness of individuals and their organizations. Fitness, then, results in the individual and corporate entities surviving and thriving.

▶ METHOD: SAME AND DIFFERENT

Purpose

Many organizational changes require a detailed analysis of sameness and difference between two parts of an organization or among individuals within a group. Such an analysis can be most helpful during mergers and acquisitions, business expansions, and reorganizations. Frequently, these situations cause persons to stereotype the "other," to exaggerate similarities to avoid conflict, or to exaggerate differences to block collaboration.

This activity provides a quick and easy way to check for fit (similarity and difference) between parts of the CAS. It helps a group analyze differences in a way that can move it toward action. We have used it to analyze relationships with clients, among team members, among strategic or tactical options, between product features, and among competitors.

This exercise is deceptively simple. The process is efficient, and the underlying concepts are relatively clear. The power of the exercise is remarkable. It provides a platform from which participants can comprehend and plan action regarding significant differences. The example at the end of this section shows how the technique was used to design a new governing structure for an academic institution.

Preparation

None required.

Process

The change agent first asks the group to identify two parts of the system that need to build or change their relationships, whether organizations, departments, teams, or individuals.

The change agent presents a simple table (Exhibit 7.1). The group then brainstorms the similarities and differences between the two parts of the system and charts them.

Exhibit 7.1. Similarities and Differences

We want to test the fit between A _____ and B _____		
A and B are the same in the following ways.	0 + −	A and B are different in the following ways.

After all similarities and differences have been identified, the change agent focuses on the differences that have been listed. As the group focuses on the list of differences, they evaluate and rank each one according to a simple scheme:

- Differences that are *neutral* with regard to the work. These may be relevant to some functions, but are irrelevant to the issue at hand. These differences should be marked with a zero (0) in the middle column.

- Differences that are *constructive* with regard to the work. These represent the dynamic tensions of difference in skills, location, focus, or experience that hold the promise of improving the quality of the end product. These differences should be marked with a plus sign (+).

- Differences that *interfere* with the work. These are the dissonances, opinions, actions, or other characteristics that disturb the productivity of the process or threaten the quality of the product. These differ-ences should be marked with a minus sign (–).

After all differences have been coded, the group turns its attention to the negative differences. After reviewing these, the group further catego-rizes them into two groups:

- *Ones that cannot be avoided.* These may be geographical separa-tion, racial or cultural variations, connections to different motiva-tors, or other distinctions that cannot be negotiated or resolved by the group itself.

- *Ones that can be addressed by the group.* These may include dif-ferences of vocabulary, understanding, and access to tools, or other avoidable differences that restrict the group's ability to do its work.

The focus of the group then turns to the negative differences that *can* be addressed. The group picks the single *one* that will be *easiest* to address. This need not be the most significant problem or the one that causes the most frequent concern. However, it should be one that the group can commit to correcting in a relatively short time period.

The group defines the actions they are all willing to commit to that will move toward resolution of this single difference. The group makes a time-limited plan and moves toward specific actions to resolve the difference. At the next meeting of the group, the members assess their actions on the single issue. What has improved? What has not improved? How might the group have acted differently to support the change? Is this difference resolved to the satisfaction of all?

If change has not been satisfactory, the group creates an altered action plan to address the same issue. If the issue has been resolved, the group turns its attention to the next easiest difference to resolve. In this way, over a period of time, the group builds fit between the two parts of the organization. Each resolved issue strengthens the cohesiveness of the group and makes the other negative differences less powerful.

At some point, the members of the group realize that most differences they identified in the first meeting are no longer relevant. The overall dynamics of the group have changed, so new self-organized structures bind the group together in spite of differences.

Example

We used this technique to work with an academic organization that was divided geographically. The college was one educational institution with one governing board and one program of instruction, but it was located on two campuses. Each campus had its own president, and the administrative and financial functions of the two campuses were quite different.

Distinctions between the campuses grew to the point at which the Board was not able to make sense of the two as one. A committee was established to investigate the problem and to recommend a new structure that would retain the benefits of the current scheme while resolving the issues.

In the first meeting of the committee, the members identified the differences between the campuses and categorized them as neutral (0), beneficial (+), and detrimental (–). Based on this list, they began to discuss the simplest possible ways to resolve the detrimental differences. The solution that was generated caused minimal organizational disruption, but provided a mechanism to resolve ongoing issues. It consisted of a management committee of presidents and deans of both campuses. The chair of the committee, one of the presidents, functioned as an all-college executive over a short list of issues that had generated negative differences in the past. The solution allowed the college to ignore the irrelevant, maintain the constructive, and resolve the destructive differences that were a natural outgrowth of one college on two campuses.

Debriefing

In discussing this activity with a group, the change agent should look for the following:

- Items that receive unusual reactions—laughter, silence, cascade of conversation. These are probably the differences that make a difference.

- Paradoxes that appear when the same factor generates both similarities and differences in the system. These issues should be further analyzed to discern what hidden differences or similarities are present.

- Points that may be based on opinion, rather than on data. These should be challenged.

- Differences in points of view among participants. ◄

This method is an example of how to check for the fit between parts of the CAS and between CASs. Improving the fit increases the chances of long-term sustainability. With this method and the other methods and concepts presented in Chapters 2 through 7, the change agent has the tools necessary to facilitate organization change from a complexity perspective. In Chapter 8 we discuss the change agent skills needed for the work.

(8)

Self-Organization and the Change Agent:
Tips for Thriving in the New Paradigm

Ⓐ CHANGE AGENT has the opportunity to influence the emerging system-wide patterns in a CAS. Change agents assess and focus energy on the conditions for self-organization: containers, significant differences, and transforming exchanges. They observe how newly formed conditions affect the new patterns that emerge. Then they begin the cycle again, assessing, intervening, and observing the conditions and the patterns of self-organization that result from the continual interaction of the system agents. As seen in Figure 8.1, the change agent is actively involved in all aspects of the self-organization cycle.

Figure 8.1. The Change Agent and the Self-Organization Cycle

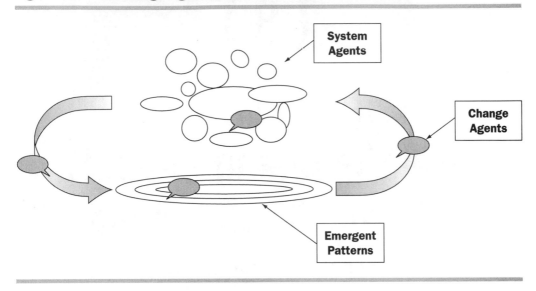

The following story shows how a small action by a change agent led to a major change in how a franchising company related to its franchisees.

▶ STORY: JUST DO IT!

Sue had been on the OD staff of a large franchising company for about a year. She had been helpful in developing new teams and new reporting relationships, and her clients wanted more understanding about organization development. They saw themselves as innovative and were resolved to deal with new issues that were emerging from their franchisees. Sue suggested that her internal clients might enjoy attending a national Organization Development Network (ODN) meeting that was being held in a nearby city.

Five members of the company attended. Three members also attended a pre-conference simulation conducted by Marv Weisbord and Associates. The attendees returned to work excited about the possibilities of constructing their own simulation. They wanted to explore the relationship between headquarters and the franchisees, which had deteriorated with rapid company expansion. One member volunteered to develop all of the technical details needed to make the simulation realistic.

The first offering of the simulation was a success. It was seen as valuable by both the headquarters staff and the franchisees who attended. The main focus was on what the franchisees needed to do to obtain approval of changes in their operations and therefore reduce the paperwork and cycle time that had become burdensome to everyone. The company now conducts the simulation as part of its annual meetings with franchisees. ◀

Lesson of the Story

When working in a CAS, where little is predictable and things are changing quickly, the best approach is the one that allows rapid integration of thought and action. Simulations and reflective practice provide opportunities to learn about change in the course of experiencing it.

This story is an example of how a small intervention by a change agent can have major unanticipated side effects. The change agent determined that the container for change, the company, was able to deal with new differences and conceived the idea of a simulation to reveal what organizational practices were blocking self-organization. The company members who went to the OD Network meeting experienced exchanges that transformed their thinking about how to improve relationships with the franchisees. The container (company) was open to the experiment they proposed, and the resulting surfacing of differences between the franchisees and headquarters and the new relationships that formed (transforming exchanges) moved the whole company to a new level of complexity that met the needs of its increasingly complex environment.

As change agents begin to use complexity science, they will be surprised at how their clients will quickly begin to take over the change process; but the shift to a complexity paradigm will also evoke many questions. In the previous chapters we identified six ways of approaching organization change from a complexity perspective:

- Change Through Connections (Not Top-Down Control)
- Adapt to Uncertainty (Not Predictable Stages of Development)
- Emerging Goals, Plans, and Structures (Not Clear, Detailed Plans or Goals)
- Amplify Difference (Not Build Consensus)
- Self-Similarity (Not Differences Between Levels)
- Success As Fit with the Environment (Not Closing the Gap with an Ideal)

In each chapter we reviewed applications for the change agent. In this chapter we summarize the major guides for change agents that emerged in the earlier chapters, including specific applications in making entry and contracting with a system, the process of assessing a system, intervening in the system, and helping the system evaluate where it is in the process of change.

We conclude this chapter with a review of the change skills needed for complexity work. The Method included at the end of the chapter, Reflection Evaluation, has broad application in a range of change initiatives.

Self-Organization and Traditional Change Methods

The effectiveness of traditional activities can be explained through the interactive process of complex adaptive systems (CAS). Following are several examples.

Storytelling. Publicly told stories about the history of the organization reveal the emergent patterns of the past. They articulate the significant differences in the history of the organization. They let members know how people have been connected in transforming exchanges, and they reinforce the organizational container by establishing one's membership in the group. However, if the stories are told privately, they establish in-group and out-group containers that interfere with system-wide self-organization.

Goal Setting. Goal setting establishes effective containers for action. Even in the uncertainty of a CAS, goals can provide coherence of commitment from a variety of members. It will not work if a group is held to long-term goals in the midst of a changing and uncertain environment.

Strategic Planning. Strategic planning can establish a feedback loop between the group's present and future status, but it will not be effective if the envisioned future is too different from the present or if the process does not establish the conditions to support self-organization toward the goals identified.

Team Building. When a team functions as a self-organizing system, it will be effective. Team-building methods shape the container, differences, and exchanges of the group to improve self-organizing processes.

Fishbowl. A fishbowl speeds up the process of self-organization because it takes the same differences that exist in the group as a whole and puts them into a smaller container. It also provides transforming exchanges that are visible to the group as they observe the interactions. A fishbowl does not work if the differences in the larger group are unclear or if they are not reflected in the members of the group in the fishbowl.

Large-Group Event. Most large-group interventions establish effective containers and lively transforming exchanges to support self-organizing processes. If the container of the intervention is not grounded in the realities of the organization, then the self-organization will not survive past the completion of the event.

Organization Design. Effective organization design will identify the conditions for self-organization for the whole. If it represents an unrealistic container, establishes impermeable boundaries within the system, or focuses on insignificant differences, then the process will be ineffective.

Conflict Resolution. At its best, conflict resolution is an example of transforming exchanges across differences. At its worst, conflict resolution focuses on similarities and damps the underlying differences that drive the behavior of the system.

Building Trust. Trust is an emergent property in a group. It cannot be built directly, but it must be the result of the self-organizing activities of the whole. Any activity that builds trust without dealing with the significant differences will provide short-lived stability for the group.

Benchmarking. Every CAS is unique. Benchmarking must include analysis of both the similarities and differences between the home system and the benchmarked system. No complex solution can be taken from one system and implemented in another, but solution options can be collected that provide ideas and examples that can destabilize an existing culture.

Best Practices. Best practices explain the specific conditions that supported self-organization in another context. Those conditions may or may not hold true in another context. Much time and energy can be lost in figuring out how they fit a new situation.

Change Agent Responsibilities

A complexity change agent is not responsible for bringing order to organizational disarray or, if the organization is without energy, to spark it to life. The key word here is *responsible*. What is expected of a change agent? And what does the change agent expect? Complexity theory at one level brings some relief as the change agent finds that order can spontaneously rise from disorder. In fact, as organizations become more organic and less mechanical, the enthusiasm for working as a change agent increases. The change agent's feelings of guilt dissipate because it is beyond his or her power to control the outcomes in a CAS.

On the other hand, a tension remains because the change agent realizes that any intervention or slightest nudge may have great impact, either positively or negatively. As a result, change agents become more attuned to what is happening in the system. They are aware that even little events and their actions can tilt the balance of a system toward stability or change.

The sequence of work of a change agent under the influence of a complexity paradigm is similar to traditional change methods. Change agents make entry into a system, establish a contract for work, gather information and collaboratively assess the system with the client, participate in interventions to move the system, and evaluate the impact of the change effort. The difference is that each stage is short, and the whole process is iterative.

- In a CAS, responsibility, authority, and decision making are distributed among system agents, although at times the leader or change agent will use authority to start the iterative process. In a hierarchical system, responsibility, authority, and decision making are vested at the top of the hierarchy.

- In a CAS, variation and experimentation are the vehicles for change. Variation is increased to increase adaptability. The mechanisms for change in a highly organized system usually involve fixed procedures and required "best practices" that decrease variation to increase control.

- In a CAS, the purpose of a change initiative is to increase system resiliency and capacity for continual adaptation. The goals of a change initiative in most organizations are to reach specified targets.

- In a CAS, the focus of the change effort is the current functioning of the organization. In most organizations, a vision of what the organization should be guides the change initiatives.

Table 8.1 summarizes the significant differences in assumptions about change.

Table 8.1. Traditional vs. CAS Assumptions About Change

Traditional	CAS
Great size and speed indicate power.	Power is not correlated with either size or speed.
The practitioner is an independent observer.	Anyone who touches (or even observes) the system influences it in some way.
The practitioner will not be transformed significantly by a consulting engagement.	The only way to transform is to be transformed.
Large transformations require large interventions.	Small changes can have enormous effects.
Systems seek equilibrium, and they are most healthy in that state.	Living systems thrive when they are poised far from equilibrium.
Interventions should be implemented one at a time.	Massive, parallel interventions push the system toward change.
Change is difficult. It requires thoughtful and informed design of an intervention.	Change is easy. It is perpetual, although not always productive or permanent.
The practitioner should be able to predict the outcome of an intervention.	Human systems are inherently unpredictable. Observe and adapt.
A snapshot description of an organization is helpful.	All meaningful patterns emerge over time, not in an instant.
Change is toward an intended end. Change models are developmental.	Change results from many causes at many different levels of analysis.
Levels of analysis require different explanatory models and interventions.	Levels are interdependent. Patterns are repeated across various scales.
Resistance is expected.	Resistance does not exist. It is attraction to an existing pattern.
Shared values give a group resilience and ability to respond to changing conditions.	A dynamic tension between shared values and differences sets the stage for adaptation.
Solutions can be generalized.	No two environments are alike. Solutions cannot be generalized.
Cooperation is good. Competition is bad.	A healthy tension between cooperation and competition is most adaptive.
Organizational power and positions are the most powerful differences.	Any dimensions of difference can reshape organizational patterns.

Entering the System

The change agent in a CAS must determine the level of organizational awareness about what is already changing. Is there an acknowledgment of the need for adaptive change? Or does the leadership want a linear process to reach specific goals following predictable steps? In the contracting process, the change agent must inquire about the change paradigm in the minds of the system agents. For example, in a recent consulting engagement, it was discovered that the group had a bad experience of being manipulated in large-group meetings. Their change paradigm did not support a large-group process at that time. We recommended a diagonal slice task force to explore ways of initiating a change process in the organization. The group decided on an appreciative inquiry approach (Watkins, in press) and planned a large-group event with input from all subgroups. The subsequent large meeting was a success.

Not all organization work requires a complexity approach. When the future is clear, stable, and predictable, and when the means to bring about change are well-known, traditional approaches may be warranted. Rational and quantitative evaluation and selection of optimal courses of action to accomplish specific objectives may be the only sensible approach.

Some of the specific actions change agents can take when developing a contract with a new client are as follows:

- Determine whether there is sufficient uncertainty and unpredictability to justify a complexity approach.

- Determine whether the container for organization change will support the self-organizing processes of identifying significant differences and transforming exchanges.

- Identify the important differences necessary for emergence and self-organization.

If your initial efforts determine that a complexity approach is appropriate, then you should consider the following specific points in the entry/contracting process:

- Enter as many levels as possible with the active involvement of the primary client.

- Determine readiness for change and whether the organization wants to achieve a better fit with its environment.

- Set realistic expectations about the degree of certainty and predictability of the change initiative. Give examples from other CASs where the end point shifted during the change process.

- Ask about the obvious sanctioned differences in the system, such as reporting hierarchy and functional specialization, and contract to explore the hidden differences.

- Contract to create or modify containers for the change process and work with transformative exchanges.

- Identify whether change is expected in the linear or nonlinear aspects of the system, or in both.

- Contract for iterative application of a short list of rules that drive behavior in the system.

Assessment

Assessment in a CAS involves asking questions, "reading" organizational patterns, and helping to identify the opportunities to respond. Assessments should be designed to explore instances of mutual causality, areas of linearity and predictability, and areas of nonlinearity and uncertainty at all levels in the organization.

Some questions that can be helpful in determining the self-organizing aspects of an organization follow:

- What important differences have not been recognized and expressed?
- What parts of the system appear to be stable?
- Where is change occurring in the container?
- What is leadership doing to set the container?
- What short list of rules governs the behavior of system agents?
- Which rule(s) could be modified to aid self-organization?
- How will outside stakeholders raise significant differences?
- What important relationships are developing?
- Do these relationships have room to grow?
- What do you imagine would happen if the system became more self-organizing?

- How autonomous are individuals and teams?
- What is the source of "energy"? Is it moving the system to self-organization?
- Do the fitness measures suggest that more or less self-organization is needed?

Table 8.2 can help the change agent identify issues that may require a CAS approach.

Table 8.2. A CAS Approach to Various Issues

Presenting Problem	CAS Interpretation	Possible Actions
High levels of fear	Insufficient transforming exchanges or unclear or too large container	Redesign feedback loops; redefine scope, membership, vision; shrink container
Risk aversion	Significant differences unclear or undefined	Articulate important differences
Perceived resistance to change	Self-organized patterns that are not productive	Identify significant differences that are represented in current patterns and incorporate or damp them in new ones
Rampant rumors	Dysfunctional feedback mechanisms	Redesign feedback systems; flood the system with reliable information
Systematic blaming	Irrelevant containers	Establish new boundaries of accountability; establish transforming exchanges among them
Too much to do, too little time	Focus on too many differences at the same time	Refocus on significant difference(s)
Unclear communications	Dysfunctional feedback and exchange systems	Redesign length, width, frequency, and medium for feedback exchange

The conditions of self-organization (container, significant differences, and transforming exchanges) frame all organizational interactions. By focusing on them, the change agent can assess and plan interventions that will shift the energy of the system toward new, more adaptive self-organizing patterns.

Intervention

A complexity-oriented change agent does not stay on the boundary and remain marginal to the system. The change agent takes a stance of complexity, stirring the pot with questions, highlighting differences in the container, creating transforming exchanges among system agents, and maintaining the containers for the work.

> CHANGE AGENTS create tension by helping the organization stay in the space between tradition (what has been successful) and surviving (by adapting to the changing environment).

In the course of raising fundamental questions, the change agent helps connect leaders and other agents. Change agents create tension by helping the organization stay in the space between tradition (what has been successful) and surviving (by adapting to the changing environment). The change agents help leaders give up their expectation of control and instead rely on the many means for transformative exchanges within a CAS. The change agent helps develop capacity for collecting and responding to information, develops trust in the informal networks, and leaves responsibility for action and change with the client. The change agent looks for small changes that can lead to big results. If appropriate, the change agent employs a tit-for-tat strategy.

Dealing with Hostility

As change agents begin to apply complexity concepts, there is likely to emerge a combination of apprehension, uncertainty, and confusion among organizational members that will seem like general hostility. The change agent can use some questions to help system agents to surface their feelings and concerns.

- How is this new experience different from your idea of how change occurs?
- How are the new ideas about change different from the ideas you hold?
- What activities will help bridge the gap between new and old ideas?
- How can we reinforce new self-organized understandings?
- What is interfering with the learning process?

- Where do you feel stuck?

- What different ideals or models about change exist in the organization?

- What activities or questions will help leverage the differences to enhance the development of common understandings?

- What common experiences can be used to synchronize learning for the group?

- What are your fears?

These questions not only assist the change agent in designing new conditions for self-organization, but the conversations that the group has around the questions begin the process of constructing the self-organizing patterns.

Developing a Container

A human CAS cannot evolve if its agents are filled with anxiety. Leaders and change agents have a role in creating a safe place, at least safe enough for system agents to take risks associated with movement and change. Accepting the unknowability of the future and letting go of the need to control are the most difficult parts, even for the change agent. Trust within the container is fundamental. It replaces the short-term focus on the bottom line. Trust affirms mutual self-interest that will survive beyond the end of the quarter.

A common understanding of purpose and relationships develops coherence and energy in the container. Plans and specific directions emerge with the continuing stirring of many diverse, simultaneous, unpredictable interactions. In the midst of all of this divergence, a common purpose and rich relationships hold the organization together into a self-organizing whole.

Being in the same container with the client makes the change agent more sensitive to the values, norms, and history of the organization. The change agent is aware of how the culture is manifested in the language, dress, and behavior of the system agents. The consultant has to find a place of similarity in order to co-evolve with the client. For example, establishing a shared vision, common approach, and mutuality in the learning process establishes a container for mutual influence. The consultant also must maintain difference with the client by raising questions and seeing other possibilities.

The telling of a *good story* enlarges the container. The accomplished storyteller knows the audience's values, concerns, and interests. For example, Tom Peters lectures to top managers with stories about entrepreneurs who dared to be wrong. His intent is to replace old containers (business models) that are not adapting to the complexity of the environment.

Choosing the *right words* will also increase the space in the container for new possibilities. For example, Southwest Airlines uses the concepts of "family" to help its employees identify with the company. Some firms find new words to express their main business. Xerox has shifted from "copies" to "document company." Kodak is broadening the base of its container by becoming the "image company." Media companies are struggling to find the right way to talk about the mergers of the technologies of TV, cable, Internet, satellite, and telephone. If a company chooses words that do not resonate with the audience's needs and values or ones that do not reflect the scope of the work, it risks losing market share.

Transforming Exchanges

Many agents feel isolated, ignored, misunderstood, and unappreciated. Often people are assigned to work groups with little agent input. Agents in such a system need to form transforming exchanges and thus create the building blocks of self-organization.

In a complex system, each agent must be connected to many other agents—both inside and outside of the system. These connections include those with customers, with the business, with the history of products, and with emerging technologies. Each of these connections provides information that allows individuals, products, and teams to evolve along with their environments.

In biological systems, the surface area of an organism determines its opportunity to make contact with other agents in the environment. The larger the surface area, the more interaction. For example, the large surface area in a human's small intestine allows maximum absorption of the food consumed.

In organizations, too, larger surface area means more connections and better "digestion" of information. Indicators of surface area are meetings, hallway conversations, networks, employee group meetings, and website hyper-links. Meaningful connections change the way relationships and patterns form. By including employees, customers, and other stakeholders in honest and respectful interactions, levels of trust and respect increase. An organization will co-evolve with its stakeholders by taking risks, not by punishing "failure," and by carrying out open dialogue. For example, Kelly (1994) suggests enhancing organizational connectivity by linking customers to other customers and choosing technologies that connect rather than isolate people from each other.

Significant Differences

Change agents are people who represent a significant difference. They bring specialized knowledge and expertise. They also bring personal qualities, such as humor, perspective, warmth, analytical rigor, and intuition. These qualities may help the group to surface differences that have remained hidden. For example, a group may be ignoring an underlying dynamic such as intra-group competition, race, gaps in technical knowledge, or educational disparities. In Lewinian terms, the system needs to be "unfrozen" so that the system agents can create new patterns. By contrast, in a CAS the system is not expected to "refreeze" into a permanent pattern.

For example, when organizing information about a system, the change agent often identifies themes accompanied by selected quotes or short stories from the system. These illustrate how system agents talk to one another and influence each other and contain the significant differences that are ready to be surfaced. These differences shape the focus of the group. They also contribute to the development of transforming exchanges by identifying which system agents need to connect with one another and which agents need to be responsible for what actions.

Evaluation

By evaluating the state of a CAS, the change agent is checking the degree to which the system is self-organizing. For example, a change agent might evaluate patterns of leadership and the ability of the system to adapt, its fitness, and the impact on the system of dealing with hidden differences. The act of evaluation itself should evolve during the interventions. Because the systems are always changing, the challenge is to find appropriate measures. The evaluations should be frequent and iterative and measure the degree of fit of the group with the organization and with other stakeholders. The results of the evaluation should make leadership patterns evident.

The Method: Reflection Evaluation, p. 149, is useful for frequent and iterative measures of how the CAS is changing. It promotes individual and group learning about what actions lead to what outcomes.

Measurement and Accountability

Many measures in contemporary organizations were developed for the model of "organization as machine." Most of these measures are not relevant for "organizations as complex adaptive systems."

From a complexity perspective, the ultimate criteria of organizational success are adaptability and sustainability in the face of environmental pressures. Measuring adaptability requires making measurements, adaptations, and new measurements repeatedly. As additional data are gathered, models and estimates are refined. In the following example, Richard Knowles (1999) found out what is important to pay attention to.

"When I was a plant manager, I kept track of the amount of time I spent each day (on a monthly average) working on the important but not urgent safety, health, and environment issues at the plant. After a while I noticed that whenever my monthly average dropped below 1.5 hours a day in this work, we had an OSHA recordable injury; I discovered that somehow I was impacting the field in this plant of 1,000 people. Over a five-year period, the only months we had an injury were those where my work dropped below 1.5 hours a day. Needless to say, I began to pay a lot of attention to this measurement."

Knowles' experience suggests that significant measures will emerge from the experience of the system agents. The measures must be related to something that is meaningful and to what systems agents actually do.

What to Measure

Measuring adaptability is difficult because most current measures of organizational outputs only indirectly measure adaptability. Subjective measures of the factors underlying organizational adaptability are helpful in getting the dialogue started. The questionnaire in Exhibit 8.1 can be administered to a group to identify areas that may be blocking adaptability. Once important areas are identified, the group is likely to suggest more objective, tangible ways to measure changes in these areas over time. Identifying areas of self-similarity of organizational levels or departments may provide a complexity index of the whole CAS, even allowing comparative measurements with other CASs on a complexity scale.

Exhibit 8.1. Adaptability Questionnaire

	Low				High
Container					
Level of trust	1	2	3	4	5
Number of teams (functional building blocks)	1	2	3	4	5
Transforming Exchanges					
Frequency of performance feedback	1	2	3	4	5
Variety of data used in feedback	1	2	3	4	5
Significant Differences					
Willing to surface hidden differences	1	2	3	4	5
Diversity of workforce	1	2	3	4	5
Roles					
Flexibility	1	2	3	4	5
Extent of cross-training	1	2	3	4	5
Leadership					
Individual decision making w/o authorization	1	2	3	4	5
Degree of coaching mentoring	1	2	3	4	5
System Knowledge					
Agent initiative in learning	1	2	3	4	5
Number of planned experiments	1	2	3	4	5
Adaptability Index (sum of all numbers)					

If the adaptability scores in Exhibit 8.1 are high (48+), it is likely that the organization has a high potential for self-organization, as it is confronted by changes in its environment. A low score (< 25) suggests that the organization will likely stay stuck in its current pattern unless there is a large outside shock to the organization. Organizations with scores in the midrange of 25 to 47 may respond if one of the dimensions is chosen as a focal point for change.

Skills for a Complexity Approach

Are any special skills needed for this work? Not much has been written in answer to this question. A change agent needs a substantial capacity for adaptation and an ability to see things from many different angles. There are three clusters of skills that are most valuable: (1) perception of reality (what is there); (2) propensity to act and seeing the results of the action; and (3) building relationships. See Exhibit 8.2 for a Self-Assessment Instrument. The instrument suggests the kind of mental model and attitudes that are necessary to function effectively in a CAS. The three dimensions of *perception, actions,* and *relationships* are discussed below.

Exhibit 8.2. Self-Assessment

	Low				High
Perception					
Awareness of readiness of system to self-organize	1	2	3	4	5
Recognize results of actions	1	2	3	4	5
Able to see phenomena from many perspectives	1	2	3	4	5
Actions					
Propensity to act	1	2	3	4	5
Sustain energy during times of ambiguity	1	2	3	4	5
Respond to unpredictable comments or behavior	1	2	3	4	5
Relationships					
Willing to amplify relationships	1	2	3	4	5
Focus on learning, not problem solving	1	2	3	4	5
Develop trusting, caring relationships	1	2	3	4	5
Complexity Skill Index (sum of all numbers)					

Perception

In a CAS, it is important that the change agent be able to perceive what is happening in the system at any given time. The change agent should look for indications of readiness to self-organize, for example, a high degree of individual initiatives and risk taking. Seeing system phenomena from several perspectives keeps the change agent from aligning with any one force for change and allows him or her to promote a high degree of interaction. Seeing the results of agent interactions (formation of a team) helps the change agent to be ready for the next iteration (team impact on other entities in the system).

THE CHANGE AGENT should look for indications of readiness to self-organize, for example, a high degree of individual initiatives and risk taking.

Actions

A change agent must be ready and willing to take action to help the system move forward with adaptation. A complexity change agent must be able to work effectively in nonlinear situations that are essentially unpredictable and full of surprises. As relationships are amplified, it is likely there will be miscommunication. For example, in discussing significant differences it is likely that system agents will give ambiguous or defensive messages. The messages may even be offensive. Different people will have different reactions to the same message. Communication is an invitation for dialogue. Differences in perspectives and beliefs provide valuable information. They are an opportunity for exploration and learning.

The change agent must maintain the energy level during times of ambiguity and frustration. A change agent's actions can be very helpful in keeping the organization from reverting to a mechanistic state with heavy dependence on leaders for direction.

Relationships

A change agent must be able to establish a trusting and caring relationship with all system agents, including leaders. These relationships must be appropriately amplified to bring out the potential of individuals in the system. Helping system agents focus on their learning will keep the change agent from trying to take over and solve the system problems.

If the agent's total score in Exhibit 8.2 is high (36+), he or she may find a complexity approach akin to the usual way of operating. A low score (< 19) may indicate that the agent is more comfortable with predictable methods in an organized system. To raise the complexity skill score it is best to pick only one of the three areas: perception, actions, or relationships. Specific feedback could be obtained from co-workers with ideas of how more skills can be developed.

The reader may also find it useful to take the Self-Diagnosis: Organization Change Framework questionnaire at the beginning of the book again. A deeper understanding of complexity concepts and methods may bring a change to one's current approach to organization change. Any shift from the left column (traditional approach) to the right column (complexity approach) may indicate movement in the respondent's mental model about change.

Summary

Complexity thinking helps the change agent gain a better comprehension of organization behavior. A complexity perspective does not give answers per se. The unpredictability in complex systems makes it impossible to find absolute answers that work in every situation. Only the questions can be carried reliably from one context to another.

The most important rule that should guide a change agent's behavior in a CAS is to maintain responsibility, authority, and decision making capacity in the local agents in the system. At times a formal leader or the change agent may need to use his or her authority to start the interactive process, but the authority should be widely distributed as soon as possible.

The change agent should watch out for colluding with restrictive practices, rigid procedures, required "best practices," and assembly-line regulations. By championing variation and experimentation, the change agent will increase the system's resiliency and capability for continual adaptation.

▶ METHOD: REFLECTION EVALUATION

Purpose

This activity supports a reflective process of evaluation that elicits the insights of all members of a group. It supports distributed control by making explicit the expectations and assessments of all individuals in a group.

We have used this process in a variety of small groups with good results. Individuals, teams, and large groups can use the process to reinforce the concept that each is a contributing agent to change and to improve communications about the critical differences that shape self-organization.

Preparation

The instructions and guidelines that accompany the form (Exhibit 8.3) should be self-explanatory. It may be necessary to rename the levels that will receive the effects of the change to match the context of the group. Be sure that all members of the group recognize that agreement is not the goal, but rather to understand the differences that exist within the group.

Process

The Reflection Evaluation process can be used productively in a variety of situations and environments. Change agents should feel free to adapt the process for their own needs. In planning to use the process, however, the following guidelines should be followed:

- The reflection process should be used at the beginning and end of various:

  - Kinds of activities, such as meetings, projects, team formation activities, and training sessions.

  - Time periods, such as hour, week, month, quarter, or year.

- The process can be used to support the work of various groups, including individuals, formal and informal teams, short- and long-term project teams, and intact work groups.

- All members of the group should participate in the Reflection Evaluation. The perspectives of leaders, guests, and permanent members all provide valuable insights.

- The process should not take much meeting time. In most circumstances, spend no more than five minutes completing the form and fifteen minutes discussing it.

- Ensure all participants that "close enough" agreement is the goal. There is no need for the whole group to come to consensus on an answer. It is much more valuable for all members to hear the perspectives of each of the others. Disagreements provide opportunities for learning and growth.

- In some situations, the form will not be completed in one sitting. Participants will state their goals, but information about outcomes will not be available until later. One person should be responsible for collecting the completed sheets and keeping them for later analysis.

- The instructions below are for a single-iteration process. (We usually format the instructions so that they fit on the one-page back of the form itself.) In larger or longer projects, however, a single iteration is only the beginning of a long-term process. Each time a group uses the form to investigate its differences, system agents will have a better sense of their emerging patterns of self-organization. Each iteration will provide more information about the dynamics of the group and the evaluation of their actions.

Reflection Process Instructions

Follow these steps to complete the Reflection Evaluation:

1. Decide who will be affected and what the goal is for each group. Describe in as few words as possible the most observable and concrete goal you can identify for each of the affected groups. Fill in the section of the form for each group you think will be affected.

   - Use N/A for not applicable when the group is not relevant to your current process.

   - Use "indirect" when the outcome is not directly related to your action.

   - Use "none" when you expect that your action will have no effect on the group.

2. When you complete a process, decide what the outcome of the action was for each of the affected groups. Describe in as few words as possible the most observable and concrete outcome you can identify for the affected groups. Complete the section of the form to indicate the outcomes you observed.

   - Use "too soon" to indicate that the intended outcomes have not had time to materialize.

   - Use "none" to indicate that there was no observed outcome on the group.

3. Determine what the next steps should be, based on the goals and observed outcomes.

4. Decide who should share the reflection on goals and outcomes and make copies of the form and arrange for the copies to be distributed.

5. After you have completed five reflection sheets in a series (for example, five meetings of the same team or five short-term projects), take some time to reflect on the whole series. Ask yourself and the group:

   - What have we learned?

   - Have our goals changed?

   - Are we personally satisfied with our progress?

   - How should we adapt to improve our work?

Exhibit 8.3. Reflection Evaluation Form

Company: _____

Reflection Process

This is form number: _____	Date: _____ Team: _____ Process: _____ Evaluator/Participant: _____	Date: _____ Team: _____ Process: _____ Evaluator/Participant: _____
Who will feel the effect of the action?	What is the goal of my (our) action?	What was the outcome of the action?
Myself		
My Team		
My Department		
The Division		
The Company		
External Customers		
What should I (we) do next?		
Who would benefit from seeing this reflection?		

Debriefing

In discussing the activity with a group, the change agent should look for:

- Indications of container definitions and how they vary from one person to another.

- Identification of transforming exchanges for individuals and the group as a whole.

- Assessments of the feedback loops that are currently in place to support continuing self-organizing processes. ◀

The Reflection Evaluation method can be used continuously in an organization in the process of setting appropriate containers, surfacing significant differences, and fostering transforming exchanges. It represents a mental model and way of being that makes self-organization a continual reality. We summarize the other perspectives and actions that are essential for working as a CAS change agent in Chapter 9.

9

Making Self-Organization a Reality:
Evolution in Organizations

OF LEFT ALONE, organizations and groups will self-organize. Their naturally occurring containers, transforming exchanges, and significant differences will shape the patterns that emerge over time for better or for worse. In the past the two most common change strategies to deal with the dynamics of self-organization have been either to constrain the dynamics or to ignore them. The purpose of this book has been to propose a third—what we believe to be a more responsible and effective-change strategy.

Some scholars and practitioners of CAS development suggest that the change agent stand by and observe as an organization self-organizes without constraint. We believe that this approach will sometimes generate adaptive behaviors and will sometimes lead to disastrous outcomes.

Adams and Adams (1999) agree. They state:

"As trusted consultants, we were not comfortable advising corporate leaders that there was no longer any need for corporate control, internal systems, and measurements or that their company would simply 'self-organize' when a problem needed to be solved. Although Wheatley's theories certainly expanded our horizons, we found that scientific theories could easily be skewed when applied to their human equivalent." (p. 52)

In contrast, the more common, machine-based approach to organizing systems has been successful historically. In this model, the conditions of self-organization have been tightly constrained by change agents and leaders so that the results could be predicted and controlled. Although successful in the past, such a command-and-control strategy is not flexible enough to work consistently in today's fast-paced organizational environment.

Lewin and Regine (2000) point out that businesses fluctuate between different states, from static to chaotic, with the zone of creativity in between. Different states are appropriate for different times. A static state is appropriate when the environment is changing little and is certain. A chaotic state is necessary when old patterns must be broken through and replaced with something new, but as yet unknown. The zone of creativity is most important when innovation is necessary (Lewin & Regine, 2000, p. 320).

We believe that the challenge is not to fall into an either/or dichotomy between abandonment and control. There are linear aspects of an organization that require treatment by the best Newtonian, mechanistic methods. There are also aspects of organization development that are unpatterned and beyond the conscious capacity to shape emergent interactions. It is possible to understand the process of self-organization and to participate as an active agent in the change process when an organization is at any place along the continuum between order and disorder.

Adams and Adams (1999) have distilled their approach to unify the mechanistic and organic approaches in the concept: "Organizations are living systems with mechanical parts." We believe that change agents need the knowledge and skills related to both Newtonian and self-organizing mechanics of change. Our effort in this text has been to explain the process of change in a self-organizing system and explain ways that the change agent can interact with the self-organizing process to help shape its path toward adaptation.

Some change agents have successfully integrated complexity theory in their practices. We have described some of their situations and decisions in previous chapters. Richard Knowles, for example, has developed a "theory of corporate sustainability that involved fluidity of structure, strength of identity, degrees of diversity and connectivity, and the depth of human reflection, and applied his thinking as a consultant to groups in the U.S. and Australia" (Petzinger, 1999, p. 192).

In this chapter we review and summarize the perspectives and activities that we believe are essential to work respectfully and effectively as an active agent for change in a CAS.

Work with the Conditions for Self-Organization

Three factors influence the self-organizing patterns in a CAS: *container, significant differences,* and *transforming exchanges.* A change to any of these conditions changes the speed, shape, vigor, and adaptability of the self-organizing process. A change agent can use these three conditions as a model to contract with client systems, assess the current patterns, intervene to shift patterns, and evaluate the effectiveness of patterns as they emerge in an active CAS. Although the change agent cannot predict outcomes of actions, he or she can experiment to determine which set of conditions is most productive for a particular system in a particular place and time.

In addition to using these three levers to influence organization change, the change agent must adopt innovative assumptions about change in organizations. Preceding chapters outlined six of these assumptions. All six are summarized below.

1. Change Through Connections (Not Top-Down Control)

Change in a self-organizing system does not come from a pre-ordained design or the top-down exercise of power. Instead, it searches and lurches its way along through the complex and massively entangled interactions of individuals and groups.

When change agents recognize this fundamental rule of self-organizing, they collect information about and seek to influence the transforming exchanges that tie system agents together into networks of adaptation. This model moves beyond self-managed teams and participative management. It speaks to the need to shape interactions to encourage mutual transformation across the system and at all levels of organization (see Table 9.1).

Table 9.1. Sources of Energy for Change

Pattern	Traditional Thinking	CAS Thinking
Perception of Situation	Change must begin and be orchestrated by the top officials in the organization	Change comes from transforming exchanges among networks of system agents at all levels simultaneously
Typical Response to Situation	Construct a change initiative focused on developing and implementing a strategic plan	Formal control is relinquished as the organization self-organizes
Usual Outcome	Constrained system with a mix of success and failure and a mix of winners and losers with a new set of problems to be solved	Organization reaches a new state, including reinstitution of necessary controls

Briggs and Peat (1999) believe the process of dialogue is the means to this end:

"It would mean opening up ourselves and our organizations to the shocks, grief, confusions, and mysteries that befall us by directly engaging the ethical, moral, and spiritual dilemmas of our activities. It would mean explicitly working with the tensions of diversity and divergences in points of view that are an inevitable part of collective activity but are now routinely turned into a mere power struggles and the uneasy truces of compromise." (pp. 73–74)

One major job of the change agent in a CAS is to establish dialogue and other forms of transforming exchanges between system agents at all levels. It is this process, not top-down control, that will lead to adaptive and long-lasting organization change.

2. Adapt to Uncertainty (Not Predictable Stages Of Development)

Self-organizing systems are inherently unpredictable. This characteristic generates creative opportunities, but it also complicates the job of the change agent. Some small interventions may result in enormous changes, and some enormous interventions may make no difference at all. In such situations, change agents must take advantage of the existing conditions for self-organization. Traditional OD interventions that depend on predictable stages of development may be useful in some constrained situations, but they cannot be relied on to predict future, system-wide patterns (see Table 9.2).

Table 9.2. Coping with Uncertainty

Pattern	Traditional Thinking	CAS Thinking
Perception of Situation	Uncertainty should be minimized through rational analysis of options	Uncertainty is an indicator that the organization has potential to self-organize
Typical Response to Situation	Use of linear methods such as problem solving	Promote uncertainty by identifying significant differences and creating transforming exchanges within a container to hold the interactions
Usual Outcome	Some situations are appropriately managed; many opportunities are lost	Organization agents identify outcomes that work, that is, they are adaptive responses to the environment

Bill's story will be informative here.

Bill was known as an autocrat. His reputation for a steel-trap mind and for a rigorous approach had intimidated many in the organization before Sally arrived on the scene.

When Sally asked Bill to consider some concepts from complexity science, he was quite skeptical. Sally used the Decision Making Under Uncertainty Model (Chapter 3) to help Bill plot the issues he faced. She asked, "Where is your department on this model? Do you want the department to develop toward more adaptability or toward more certainty? What actions do you want to take?"

Bill saw that he defined all of his department's issues in the "rational" section—issues with a high degree of certainty and few alternatives. Of course, that perspective was true for some issues, but not all. He began to see that it would be useful to move issues such as interdepartmental relations and resource sharing into the "self-organizing" domain. He realized that he needed to use approaches that were more suitable to adaptation and self-organization.

By providing new constructs to people like Bill, who was firmly stuck in old patterns and ways of thinking, complexity science helps loosen controls and sparks new ideas and diversity of views, even in those who prefer the machine model.

Leaders and change agents must learn and help others learn to assess the amount of uncertainty in a particular situation and to respond appropriately.

3. Emerging Goals, Plans, and Structures (Not Clear, Detailed Plans or Goals)

The future of a CAS emerges from the raw materials of the present. Goals, plans, and structures are necessary for effective adaptation, but they cannot be determined in a vacuum. The change agent and leaders must understand and work within the capacities and constraints of the interactive system.

Short lists of simple rules help bring coherence to the self-organizing process. Stories and experiments allow for mid-course corrections as the system and its environment evolve. Like schools of fish or growing spider plants, an organizational CAS shapes its behavior by establishing core structural principles and then adapting to local situations. The change agent can facilitate this process by helping the system articulate the conditions in which the system self-organizes (see Table 9.3).

Table 9.3. Constructing Goals, Plans, and Structures

Pattern	Traditional Thinking	CAS Thinking
Perception of Situation	Detailed objectives, plans, and structures are necessary to manage the organization	A short list of simple rules is needed to bring coherence to the self-organizing process
Typical Response to Situation	Much effort is put into specification of how authority is distributed	The rules are identified and modified
Usual Outcome	The complicated organizational plans and structures interfere with responding to internal and external customers	Effective behaviors and direction emerge and are recognized by organization leaders

Self-organization occurs in an environment in which successful divisions of labor and routines not only emerge but also self-adjust in response to environmental changes. The climate encourages rapid evolution toward higher fitness, not mastering the art of planning and monitoring work flows. Self-organization is not the same as a self- managed team, or empowerment, or a flat organization chart. It is not laissez-faire management. Instead, it means *to commit to guiding the evolution of behaviors and interactions instead of specifying effective behavior in advance, "then encourage the agents to conform to the standard"* (Anderson, 1999, p. 120).

> **SELF-ORGANIZATION is not the same as a self- managed team, or empowerment, or a flat organization chart. It is not laissez-faire management.**

4. Amplify Difference (Not Build Consensus)

Significant differences are the engine for change in an organizational CAS. When ignored, differences disrupt the self-organizing process. When surfaced and incorporated into the emerging patterns, difference lends the power and flexibility to the process and the patterns that emerge (see Table 9.4).

Table 9.4. Managing Differences

Pattern	Traditional Thinking	CAS Thinking
Perception of Situation	Diverging opinions are necessary and useful as a prelude to converging on consensus	Significant differences are amplified. Consensus is not required
Typical Response to Situation	Creativity session; brainstorming is encouraged until leaders determine that it is time to reach consensus	Continuous process of interacting and action around significant differences, anticipating that learning will occur
Usual Outcome	Decisions are made that are not supported by everyone in the organization	Decisions are made as the next evolutionary step for the system becomes clear

Some organizational leaders resist diversity of ideas by prohibiting members from questioning the organization's core values and assumptions. This generates homogeneous systems, which have only a few narrow and rigid options for responding to complex issues. Such organizations risk becoming so inflexible and brittle that the entire organization can lose its ability to adapt (Roos, 1997). The ultimate outcome may be a loss of market share or bankruptcy. For example, the leaders of a training department of a company made meeting the needs of company executives a priority. Dissenting opinions of the training staff were squelched, and all communications with the executives had to be channeled through the training department leaders. The functions of the training department were soon outsourced after all of the creative people left.

Change agents can use transforming exchanges to identify significant differences and connect across them to move the system toward creative adaptive responses.

5. Self-Similarity (Not Difference Between Levels)

All levels and parts of a CAS are intimately linked together. Patterns that appear at one place are likely to appear at others. This self-similarity serves two functions. First, it gives coherence and meaning to the system patterns as a whole. Second, it provides the motivation for the disparate parts of the organization to come together into a self-organizing unit (see Table 9.5).

Table 9.5. Diffusing the Change

Pattern	Traditional Thinking	CAS Thinking
Perception of Situation	Each part of the organization requires a different change strategy	There is a similarity across all levels of a CAS
Typical Response to Situation	Conduct separate change initiatives for each level and/or function	Start small changes in many parts of the organization and link them to the whole
Usual Outcome	Parts of organization optimize, but there is a lack of coherence in the whole	Adoption of changes that fit the particular needs of each part and give coherence to the whole

Emergent self-similarity in an organization means that different strategies or change models are not necessary for different levels of organization. Individual, dyad, small-group, departmental, organization-wide, and industry-wide change all self-organize through the same mechanisms. Although the containers, differences, and exchanges are different in size and content, the underlying mechanism is identical.

As an example of a common strategy, Sherman and Schultz (1998) tell the story of Aspen Mountaineering, a small company in Colorado that started out with a single idea: Offer the finest-quality mountaineering equipment. The company hired only mountaineers as salespeople. They were instructed to be absolutely honest with customers, even if that meant telling the customer that the prices were too high or that they were buying more than they needed. There was a lot of competition in town. Aspen had a poor location. It opened for business in the off-season. In spite of all these negatives, Aspen was the number one mountaineering store from the day it opened its doors. Everything else emerged from the one principle of quality service.

The role of the change agent is to help organizations recognize the similarities that provide coherence and to support emergence of new repeating patterns when the old ones cease to be useful.

6. Success As Fit with the Environment (Not Closing the Gap with an Ideal)

In an adaptive system, no absolute measures of success exist. Instead, success is defined as the ability to transform to match changing circumstances. As an organization recognizes this principle of complexity, it makes explicit the goal of focusing on significant differences and engaging in transforming exchanges to support adaptation (see Table 9.6).

Table 9.6. Defining Success

Pattern	Traditional Thinking	CAS Thinking
Perception of Situation	Organization is successful if it reaches its goals	Success is ability to transform to match changing circumstances
Typical Response to Situation	All actions are directed toward goal achievement	Agents determine local changes that gain the greatest immediate improvement
Usual Outcome	Short-term survival may be assured at the expense of long-term sustainability	Organization is flexible and able to adapt for long-term sustainability

Adaptation on a rugged landscape is not about reaching the highest peak. Often the most successful tactic is to make local changes that gain the greatest immediate improvement. Adaptation occurs when agents are free to make their own connections.

In his study of small- and medium-sized companies, Petzinger (1999) found that the successful companies put employees in charge of making their own knowledge connections. Free of institutional constraints, individuals were able to make the connections that made the most sense. The number of hyper-linked roles was an indicator of the individual's fit with the environment and contribution to the organization.

For example, a company called Great Harvest, a franchise of small bread-making companies, encourages the franchisees to install and test custom solutions in their various sites. The company fosters networking and connections with other innovative sites. Petzinger (1999) concludes from this that "People must hunt for their own connections, because it is in the chase as well as the capture that learning and organization occur. The connections that people make in the search for knowledge are most often the connections on which they rely to turn information into action" (p. 162).

The role of the change agent is to help an organization reflect on this process and to keep the goal of adaptation firmly in mind.

Conclusion

We have presented a model of change based on an underlying theory of self-organization and its applications to change in organizations. In some ways the approach matches basic assumptions of organization change efforts, and in some ways it challenges them.

The model and its application form an integrated image of what it means to work productively in a system that is continually self-organizing.

As the future unfolds for business and industry, the need for constant adaptation can only become more urgent. It is likely that these concerns will grow in areas of communication technology, public health, population migrations, and scarcity of raw materials. As change agents and leaders seek to influence their organizations, their efforts will be amplified as they develop an understanding of the mechanics of complex adaptive systems and practice the skills needed to facilitate self-organization.

In this book, we have shared the concepts and tools that we have found most helpful in navigating the complex and nonlinear interactions of complex adaptive organizations. We hope that you find them helpful in the journeys of change with your organizations and those of your clients.

Continuing the Co-Evolution

The application of complexity to organization change is still in its infancy. The theories, models, and techniques that will integrate new science learning into the toolkit of the change agent are in the early stages of self-organization. We hope that this book is a significant step in the process and that readers will join us to become active agents in this process of emergent learning.

Before beginning the work together that led to this book, we each dealt with our own conditions for learning. We worked within different containers using our own studies, histories, and client environments to set the scope of our learnings. Working together stretched the container for our learning. The process of talking and writing uncovered our differences and established transforming exchanges between us as authors and practitioners. People who reviewed and provided feedback on the book before its publication expanded, again, the container for self-organization. The significant differences they recognized and the feedback they provided enriched the emerging patterns that are represented on these pages. This book is the result of those self-organizing processes among us as authors and reviewers.

Our hope is that you, too, will become an active agent in this self-organizing process by joining with us to expand, critique, apply, test, and evaluate the concepts and tools presented here. As the container expands to include readers of this book, there will be no shortage of significant differences in expectations and understanding. Each reader, we hope, will recognize how his or her understandings and actions compare and contrast with those presented here. To support the self-organizing process, however, the third condition must be in place. We must establish a method of exchange that will allow each of us as agents in this system to transform and be transformed by others.

To establish an efficient means of transforming exchange, we have established an electronic forum at *www.complexOD.com*. This site, available March 1, 2001, will include:

- Sources of information related to CAS and organization change;
- Tools and instruments;

- Links to related websites;

- Stories about these and other applications of CAS to organization change; and

- Opportunities for individuals to share their insights by publishing papers online, joining online conversations, and asking practical and theoretical questions.

We welcome your participation and promise to support your individual contributions and the emerging work of the group. All contributions will be acknowledged, because we recognize that we are all potential change agents in this complex and self-organizing field at the edge of traditional organization development. We never know what might emerge from the next iteration!

References

Adams, W.A., & Adams, C. (1999). *The whole systems approach.* Provo, UT: Executive Excellence.

Anderson, P. (1999). Seven levers for guiding the evolving enterprise. In J.H. Clippinger III (Ed.), *The biology of business* (pp. 113–152). San Francisco: Jossey-Bass.

Axelrod, R. (1997). *The complexity of competition and cooperation.* Princeton, NJ: Princeton University Press.

Baskin, K. (1998). *Corporate DNA: Learning from life.* Woburn, MA: Butterworth-Heinemann.

Baskin, K. (1998, October/November). Running a business as a complex adaptive system. *The Inner Edge,* pp. 25–28.

Blanchard, K., & Johnson, S. (1982). *The one minute manager.* New York: William Morrow.

Briggs, J., & Peat, F.D. (1990). *The turbulent mirror.* New York: HarperCollins.

Briggs, J., & Peat, F.D. (1999). *Seven life lessons of chaos.* New York: HarperCollins.

Brown, L.D. (1980). Planned change in underorganized systems. In T.G. Cummings (Ed.), *Systems theory for organization development* (pp. 181–203). New York: John Wiley & Sons.

Bunker, B., & Alban, B.T. (1996). *Large group interventions: Engaging the whole system for rapid change.* San Francisco: Jossey-Bass.

Cameron, K.S. (1997). *Techniques for making organizations effective: Some popular approaches.* Washington, DC: National Academy Press.

Chan Allen, R. (1998). *Diversity systems matrix.* Unpublished paper.

Clippinger, J.H. (Ed.). (1999). *The biology of business.* San Francisco: Jossey-Bass.

Dooley, K. (1996). A nominal definition of complex adaptive systems. *The Chaos Network, 8*(1), 2–3.

Dooley, K. (1997). A complex adaptive systems model of organizational change. *Nonlinear Dynamics, Psychology, and Life Sciences, 1*(1), 69–97.

Eisenhardt, K.M., & Galunic, D.C. (2000, January/February). Coevolving: At last, a way to make synergies work. *Harvard Business Review,* pp. 91–102.

Eoyang, G. (1997). *Coping with chaos: Seven simple tools.* Cheyenne, WY: Lagumo Publishing.

Eoyang, G.H. (2000). *Conditions for self-organization in human systems.* Unpublished doctoral dissertation, Union Institute, Cincinnati, Ohio.

Frederick, W.C. (1998, December). Creatures, corporations, communities, chaos, complexity: A naturological view of the corporate role. *Business & Society,* pp. 358–360.

Garr, D. (1999). *IBM redux: Lou Gerstner and the business turnaround of the decade.* New York: HarperCollins.

Gersick, C.J.G. (1991). Revolutionary change theories: A multi-level exploration of the punctuated equilibrium paradigm. *Academy of Management Review, 16,* 10–36.

Ghoshal, S., & Bartlett, C.A. (1995, January/February). Changing the role of top management: Beyond structure to processes. *Harvard Business Review,* pp. 86–96.

Gleick, J. (1988). *Chaos: Making a new science.* New York: Viking/Penguin.

Goldstein, J. (1994). *The unshackled organization.* New York: Productivity Press.

Guastello, S. (1995). *Chaos, catastrophe, and human affairs: Applications of nonlinear dynamics to work, organizations, and social evolution.* Mahwah, NJ: Lawrence Erlbaum.

Hagel, J., III. (1994). Fallacies in organizing for performance. *McKinsey Quarterly, 2,* 97–106.

Hammer, M., & Champy, J. (1994). *Reengineering the corporation: A manifesto for business revolution.* New York: Harper Business.

Herzberg, F., Mausner, B., & Snyderman, B. (1959). *The motivation to work.* New York: John Wiley & Sons.

Heyde, M.L. (2000, April). Unit one. *Fast Company,* p. 102.

Hock, D. (1998). *An epidemic of institutional failure.* Keynote Address at ODN Annual Conference, New Orleans, Louisiana.

Holman, P., & Devane, T. (1999). *The change handbook: Group methods for shaping the future.* San Francisco: Berrett-Koehler.

Hurst, D. (1995). *Crisis and renewal: Meeting the challenge of organizational change (The management of innovation and change series).* Boston, MA: Harvard Business School Press.

Kauffman, S. (1993). *The origins of order: Self- organization and selection in evolution.* Oxford, England: Oxford University Press.

Kauffman, S. (1995). *At home in the universe.* Oxford, England: Oxford University Press.

Kelly, K. (1994). *Out of control.* Reading, MA: Addison-Wesley.

Kelly, S., & Allison, M. (1999). *The complexity advantage: How the science of complexity can help your business achieve peak performance.* New York: McGraw-Hill.

Kelso, J. (1995). *Dynamic patterns: The self-organization of brain and behavior.* Cambridge, MA: MIT Press.

Kiel, L.D. (1994). *Managing chaos and complexity in government: A new paradigm for managing change, innovation, and organizational renewal.* San Francisco: Jossey-Bass.

Lewin, K. (1951). *Field theory in social science.* New York: Harper & Row.

Lewin, R., & Regine, B. (2000). *The soul at work: Complexity theory and business.* New York: Simon & Schuster.

Lissack, M., & Roos, J. (1999). *The next common sense: Mastering corporate complexity through coherence.* London: Nicholas Brealey.

Manville, B. (1999). Complex adaptive knowledge management. In J.H. Clippinger (Ed.), *The biology of business* (pp. 89–112). San Francisco: Jossey-Bass.

Marshak, R.J., & Katz, J.H. (1999). Covert processes: A look at the hidden dimensions of group dynamics. In *Reading Book for Human Relations Training* (8th ed.), (pp. 251–257). Alexandra, VA: NTL Institute for Applied Behavioral Sciences.

McKelvey, W. (1998, June). *Thwarting faddism at the edge of chaos: On the epistemology of complexity research.* Paper presented at the Workshop on Complexity and Organization, Brussels, Belgium.

Michaels, M. (1998). *Chaos: A 10 year collision with OD values.* Presented at ODN Annual Conference, New Orleans, Louisiana.

Morgan, G. (1997). *Imaginization.* San Francisco: Berrett-Koehler.

Olson, E.E. (1992). Opening to the change process: The transcendent function. In M. Stein & J. Hollwitz (Eds.), *Psyche at work* (pp. 156–173). Wilmette, IL: Chiron Publications.

Owen, H. (1997). *Open space technology: A user's guide.* San Francisco: Berrett-Koehler.

Peters, T., & Waterman R.H. (1982). *In search of excellence.* New York: Harper & Row.

Petzinger, T., Jr. (1999). *The new pioneers.* New York: Simon & Schuster.

Quinn, R., & Cameron, K. (1988). *Paradox and transformation.* Cambridge, MA: Ballinger.

Roos, J. (1997). *The poised organization: Navigating effectively on knowledge landscapes.* Paper presented at the Strategy and Complexity Seminar, London School of Economics, London, England.

Schein, E. (1999). *Process consultation revisited: Building the helping relationship.* Reading, MA: Addison-Wesley.

Seashore, C.N., Seashore, E.W., & Weinberg, G.M. (1992). *The art of giving and receiving feedback.* Columbia, MD: Bingham House Books.

Senge, P. (1990). *The fifth discipline: The art & practice of the learning organization.* New York: Doubleday.

Senge, P., Kleiner, A., Roberts, C., Ross, R., Roth, G., & Smith, B. (1994). *The fifth discipline fieldbook: Strategies and tools for building a learning organization.* New York: Doubleday.

Senge, P., Kleiner, A., Roberts, C., Ross, R., Roth, G., & Smith, B. (1999). *The dance of change.* New York: Doubleday.

Sherman, H., & Schultz, R. (1998). *Open boundaries.* Reading, MA: Perseus Books.

Stacey, R.D. (1992). *Managing in the unknowable: Strategic boundaries between order & chaos in organizations.* San Francisco: Jossey-Bass.

Thomas, K.W., & Kilmann, R.H. (1974). *Thomas-Kilmann conflict mode instrument.* Tuxedo, NY: Xicom.

Vaill, P. (1989). *Managing as a performing art.* San Francisco: Jossey-Bass.

Van de Ven, A., & Garud, R. (1994). The coevolution of technical and institutional events in the development of an innovation. In J. Baum & J. Singh (Eds.), *Evolutionary dynamics of organizations* (pp. 425–443). New York: Oxford University Press.

Waldrop, M.M. (1992). *Complexity: The emerging science at the edge of order and chaos.* New York: Simon & Schuster.

Waldrop, M.M. (1996, October/November). The trillion dollar vision of Dee Hock. *Fast Company,* pp. 2–9.

Watkins, J.M. (2001). *Appreciative inquiry: Change at the speed of imagination.* San Francisco: Jossey-Bass/Pfeiffer.

Weick, K. (1977). *The social psychology of organizing.* Reading, MA: Addison-Wesley.

Weisbord, M.R. (1989, Winter). Redesigning non-routine work. *Productive Workplaces, 1,* 1–4.

Wheatley, M.J. (1992). *Leadership and the new science.* San Francisco: Berrett-Koehler.

Wilber, K. (1998). *The essential Ken Wilber: An introductory reader.* Boston, MA: Shambhala.

Youngblood, M. (1997). *Life at the edge of chaos.* Dallas, TX: Perceval Publishing.

Zimmerman, B., Lindberg, C., & Plsek, P. (1998). *Edgeware: Insights from complexity science for health care leaders.* Irving, TX: VHA.

Zohar, D. (1997). *Rewiring the corporate brain.* San Francisco: Berrett-Koehler.

About the Authors

Ed **Olson** is an organization development and workforce diversity consultant and a former professor of management and organizational behavior. Earlier he was a survey researcher and professor of information science. His academic background includes the study of philosophy, government, pastoral counseling, and applied behavioral science. He is a member of the Organization Development Network and the NTL Institute of Applied Behavioral Science and serves as an adjunct faculty member in the Executive Leadership Program at George Washington University. He has written in the areas of leadership, management tools, workforce diversity, and provision of information services. His major clients have included the Food and Drug Administration; the U.S. General Accounting Office; Digital Equipment Corporation; the Diversity Institute of Bermuda; Texaco, Inc.; the National Multi-Cultural Institute; the Delphi Network; the Department of Housing and Urban

Development; and the Defense Information Systems Agency. Ed lives in Columbia, Maryland, and Longville, Minnesota.

Glenda Holladay Eoyang is president of Chaos Limited, Inc., a consulting firm that specializes in applications of complex adaptive systems theory to the behavior of human systems. Her life roles have included student of the liberal arts, high school science and math teacher, instructional designer, entrepreneur, researcher, and organization change agent. Her current interests include strategic and policy planning for government, healthcare reform, information systems integration and design, and organizational transformation. Her first book, *Coping with Chaos: Seven Simple Tools* (Lagumo, 1997), helps first-line managers act responsibly in complex systems. Her time is spent providing training, consulting, and coaching services to business and industry and researching behaviors of human CASs. In all walks of life, Glenda seeks to bridge the worlds of theory and practice to improve the experience and performance of individuals and groups. Glenda lives in Circle Pines, Minnesota.

The authors can be contacted through their website: *www.complexOD.com.*

About the Editors

William J. Rothwell, Ph.D. is professor of human resource development in the College of Education at The Pennsylvania State University, University Park. He is also president of Rothwell and Associates, a private consulting firm that specializes in a broad array of organization development, human resource development, performance consulting and human resource management services.

Dr. Rothwell has authored, co-authored, edited, or co-edited numerous publications, including *Practicing Organization Development* (with R. Sullivan and G. McLean, Jossey-Bass/Pfeiffer, 1995). Dr. Rothwell's latest publications include *The ASTD Reference Guide to Workplace Learning and Performance*, 3rd ed., 2 vols. (with H. Sredi, HRD Press, 2000); *The Competency Toolkit*, 2 vols (with D. Dubois, HRD Press, 2000); *Human Performance Improvement: Building Practitioner Competence* (with C. Hohne and S. King, Gulf Publishing, 2000); *The Complete Guide to Training Delivery: A Competency-Based*

Approach (with S. King and M. King, Amacom, 2000); *Building In-House Leadership and Management Development Programs* (with H. Kazanas, Quorum Books, 1999); *The Action Learning Guidebook* (Jossey-Bass/Pfeiffer, 1999); and *Mastering the Instructional Design Process,* 2nd ed. (with H. Kazanas, Jossey-Bass/Pfeiffer, 1998).

Dr. Rothwell's consulting client list includes thirty-two companies from the *Fortune* 500.

Roland **Sullivan** has worked as an organization development (OD) pioneer with nearly eight hundred organizations in ten countries and virtually every major industry.

Mr. Sullivan specializes in the science and art of systematic and systemic change, executive team building, and facilitating Whole System Transformation Conferences—large interactive meetings with from three hundred to fifteen hundred people.

Mr. Sullivan has taught courses in OD at seven universities, and his writings on OD have been widely published. With Dr. Rothwell and Dr. McLean, he was co-editor of *Practicing OD: A Consultant's Guide* (Jossey-Bass/Pfeiffer, 1995).

For over two decades, Mr. Sullivan has served as chair of the OD Institute's Committee to Define Knowledge and Skills for Competence in OD and was a recent recipient of the Outstanding OD Consultant of the World award from the OD Institute.

Mr. Sullivan's current professional learning is available at *www.changeagent.net.*

Kristine **Quade** is an independent consultant who combines her background as an attorney with a master's degree in organization development from Pepperdine University, and years of experience as both an internal and external OD consultant.

Ms. Quade draws from experiences in guiding teams from divergent areas within corporations and across many levels of executives and employees. She has facilitated leadership alignment, culture change, support system alignment, quality process improvements, organizational redesign, and the creation of clear strategic intent that results in significant bottom-line results. A believer in whole systems change, she has developed the expertise to facilitate groups ranging in size from eight to two thousand in the same room for a three-day change process.

Recognized as the 1996 Minnesota Organization Development Practitioner of the Year, Ms. Quade teaches in the master's programs at Pepperdine University and the University of Minnesota at Mankato and the master's and doctoral programs at the University of St. Thomas in Minneapolis. She is a frequent presenter at the Organization Development National Conference and also at the International OD Congress and the International Association of Facilitators.

Index